More praise for *When Dieting Becomes Dangerous*

"A remarkable synthesis of clinical wisdom and contemporary research. Patients and their family members will derive great benefit from its compassionate tone and practical suggestions. This book will surely become a pivotal resource in years to come." —Kathryn J. Zerbe, author of *The Body Betrayed: A Deeper Understanding of Women, Eating Disorders, and Treatment*

"*When Dieting Becomes Dangerous* contains all the essential information that families and sufferers need to have to obtain a basic understanding of anorexia and bulimia." —Laura J. Weisberg, Duke University Medical Center and Harvard Medical School

"I highly recommend this book, which is modest in size but profound in concept, based on vast clinical wisdom, and accessible to a diverse audience." —Diane Mickley, M.D., founder and director of the Wilkins Center for Eating Disorders, Greenwich, Connecticut

"This is a remarkably readable compendium summarizing the state-of-the-art, compassionate approach to these modern scourges. If you read one book on eating disorders, let it be this wonderful primer." —Timothy D. Brewerton, Medical University of South Carolina

when dieting becomes dangerous

When Dieting Becomes Dangerous

A Guide to Understanding and Treating Anorexia and Bulimia

Deborah Marcontell Michel, Ph.D., & Susan G. Willard, L.C.S.W.

With a Foreword by Arthur Crisp, M.D., D.Sc.

Yale University Press

New Haven and London

Published with assistance from the Yale University Press Mary Cady Tew Memorial Fund.

Designed by Nancy Ovedovitz and set in Swift Light type by Tseng Information Systems. Printed in the United States of America by Vail-Ballou Press.

Library of Congress Cataloging-in-Publication Data
Michel, Deborah Marcontell, 1964–
When dieting becomes dangerous : a guide to understanding and treating anorexia and bulimia / Deborah Marcontell Michel, Susan G. Willard ; with a foreword by Arthur Crisp.
p. cm.   Includes bibliographical references and index.
ISBN 0-300-09232-6 (cloth : alk. paper) — ISBN 0-300-09233-4 (pbk. : alk. paper)
1. Bulimia.   2. Anorexia nervosa.   3. Women—Mental health.   4. Eating disorders.
I. Willard, Susan G., 1945–   II. Title.
RC552.B84 M53   2002   616.85'26—dc21   2002069139

A catalogue record for this book is available from the British Library.

The paper in this book meets the guidelines for permanence and durability of the Committee on Production Guidelines for Book Longevity of the Council on Library Resources.

10   9   8   7   6   5   4   3   2   1

We dedicate this book to all the patients who have sought recovery with us. It has been a privilege to accompany them on their courageous journey and to witness their discovery of themselves. We have learned most of what we know from them.

contents

Appendixes

Severe eating disorders, as defined here, are common. The phobic fear of fat that underwrites them is widespread in the female population of the Western world. Many women live with it as a powerful factor within their makeup and social life without developing major or overt eating disorders. Others are not so fortunate. Bulimia nervosa can erupt and become a source, often secret, of longstanding social handicap and misery. Anorexia nervosa is among the most serious of the mental illnesses in terms of its crippling physical, social, and psychological effects and potentially fatal outcome. At the least, it reflects a significant compromise with suicide, as all physical growth and the psychological and social consequences that flow from such growth are aborted.

As attempted biological solutions to existential problems, often buttressed by fearful denial, these disorders demand genuine caring and professional expertise of the highest order if help is to be provided. The authors of this book are steeped in this perspective, and it is reflected in their text. The pages are replete with clinical experience and common sense, showing health care at its empirical best. The diagnostic approach is adopted for

its heuristic value, and its multidisciplinary origins are empha-
sized. Eating disorders in males are not neglected.

Here also is a publisher wise enough to encourage a text that
is both at the cutting edge for the professional and eminently
readable by the layperson. I am delighted to write this foreword
to such a worthwhile contribution to the literature.

Arthur Crisp, M.D., D.Sc.
Professor of Psychological
Medicine, Emeritus
University of London

This book is written from a developmental perspective with the intent of assisting individuals with eating disorders, and those who care about them, in understanding these potentially devastating illnesses. More specifically, our clinical experience has alerted us to the need to help all those affected by eating disorders to understand the symptoms, the possible causes, and potentially successful treatment.

These pages represent a compilation of our knowledge, which is based on scientific research as well as years of experience in treating eating disordered individuals and their families. Our goal is to provide practical, "what-to-do" information for not only persons with eating disorders but also their families, friends, teachers, school counselors, and coaches. Contact information for various resources and organizations is given to assist readers in locating help. We recognize the importance of addressing eating disorders in males and have therefore outlined the special issues involved in their treatment. Finally, we have included a chapter aimed at health care professionals who do not specialize in eating disorders. Having consulted with such professionals over the years, we thought providing practical information for the nonspecialist was important.

As we wrote this book, we endeavored to succinctly present information that is essential to understanding eating disorders. Simple overviews are therefore provided on the basics of anorexia and bulimia. For those wanting more detailed information, references are given throughout the book and in the appendix entitled Supplemental Readings. Binge-eating disorder is touched upon only briefly, as it is beyond the scope of our book to present material that explains the development and treatment of this disorder and its associated condition of obesity. In addition, we do not discuss the special needs of children with eating disorders, although we include appropriate references.

Our chapters utilize a user-friendly, question-and-answer type format. There is some overlap because of the natural relatedness of the material, and also to remind readers of points made elsewhere. We strongly suggest that readers examine *all* chapters in order to appreciate the complex issues involved for patients, family members, friends, and health care professionals. Since the majority of eating disordered individuals are female, we address the afflicted population in the feminine gender, except in the chapter on eating disorders in males.

Please Note:
While our goal is to increase knowledge and comprehension of these disorders, we emphasize that only health care professionals can diagnose and treat eating disorders. This book is not intended as a substitute for professional health care.

D.M.M.

S.G.W.

acknowledgments

We are grateful to the following colleagues who assisted us in identifying resources on eating disorders: Fernando Fernández-Aranda, Ph.D.; Jean Chambry, M.D.; Ricardo Dalle Grave, M.D.; Bryan Lask, M.D.; and Walter Vandereyecken, M.D. We also thank Diane Mickley, M.D., for her generous feedback on the medical portions of the text.

when dieting becomes dangerous

one

Introduction

Historically, anorexia nervosa and bulimia nervosa may have ex-
isted in some form since the days of "starving saints" and Roman
vomitoriums. Yet not until 1973, when Hilde Bruch published
her classic text entitled *Eating Disorders: Obesity, Anorexia Nervosa,
and the Person Within,* did anorexia become widely recognized as
a psychological disorder. Bulimia did not receive much attention until the late 1970s, and in fact was not even given a distinct name until Gerald Russell coined the term *bulimia nervosa*
in 1979.

Today eating disorders constitute a major health concern. According to the National Eating Disorders Organization, between
5 million and 10 million girls and women, and 1 million boys
and men, have some type of eating disorder. The American Psychiatric Association reports that more than 90 percent of those
who have a diagnosis of anorexia or bulimia are female. In addition, there is evidence of an increasing prevalence of eating disorders, especially in countries that are more "Westernized" or
"Americanized" in terms of cultural ideas of beauty and societal
pressures to be thin. Complicating matters further, the options
and resulting pressures on young women with regard to educa-

tion and career are greater than in decades past, while the traditional values of success based on marriage and children prevail as well.

Our young women are supposed to do it all: be thin and beautiful; have husbands and children; have professions, power, and money. In addition, our culture allows and promotes greater sexual freedom for women and girls, a phenomenon of our times that generates anxiety and fear around growing up. Thus, we see a frightening physical obsession begin to develop in girls as young as eight or nine years of age. The end product is that many girls and young women choose dieting as an imagined solution to their problems. This misguided attempt at coping may well lead to eating disorders.

Eating disorders are complicated psychiatric illnesses in which food is used to help deal with unsettling emotions and difficult life issues. When the suspicion or realization of an eating disorder hits, many questions arise. We attempt to answer some of them as simply as is possible for such multidimensional disorders. Chapter 2 describes the diagnosis of eating disorders, the emotional features that are often seen, and the medical complications that may be present. Warning signs and symptoms are included. Chapter 3 provides general information on the typical characteristics — age, race, and level of education — of people with eating disorders. Chapter 4 explains the multiple factors that contribute to the development of an eating disorder. These include biological factors, sociocultural factors, individual personality characteristics, and family characteristics. Chapter 5 advocates a multidisciplinary approach to the treatment of eating disorders, and each professional's role is examined. We also give information on getting and staying well, treatment outcomes, and how one can assess quality and level of care. We raise the matter of insurance, as well. In Chapter 6 we give practical information and general advice to concerned individuals on their roles in effective intervention and treatment of someone with an eating disorder. In Chapter 7 we discuss the similarities of and differences between males and females in the development and treatment of eating disorders. The final chapter, intended for nonspecialist physicians, dentists, mental health professionals, and nutritionists, gives basic information on the assessment and care of persons with eating disorders. References for more detailed information are included.

When Dieting Becomes Dangerous can be used as a reference book dealing with major questions about the development, diagnosis, and treatment of anorexia and bulimia. It will help you understand these disorders, and know what to do if you suspect that you, or someone you care about, has one of these illnesses. Our book can also be used to obtain advanced references for a more thorough understanding of these and related disorders. Finally, it can put you in touch with organizations that offer help.

Selected Bibliography

Agras, W. S. (1987). *Eating disorders: Management of obesity, bulimia, and anorexia nervosa.* New York: Pergamon Press.

American Psychiatric Association (1994). *Diagnostic and statistical manual of mental disorders* (4th ed.). Washington, D.C.: Author.

Bemporad, J. R. (1996). Self-starvation through the ages: Reflections on the pre-history of anorexia nervosa. *International Journal of Eating Disorders, 19,* 217–237.

Bruch, H. (1973). *Eating disorders: Obesity, anorexia nervosa, and the person within.* New York: Basic Books.

Crichton, P. (1996). Were the Roman emperors Claudius and Vitellius bulimic? *International Journal of Eating Disorders, 19,* 203–207.

Eating Disorders Awareness and Prevention. (1998). *How to help a friend with eating and body image issues.* Seattle: Author.

Garner, D. M., Garfinkel, P. E., Schwartz, D., & Thompson, M. (1980). Cultural expectations of thinness in women. *Psychological Reports, 47,* 483–491.

Leon, G. R., Carroll, K., Chernyk, K. B., & Finn, S. (1985). Binge eating and associated habit patterns with college student and identified bulimic populations. *International Journal of Eating Disorders, 4*, 43–57.

Nasser, M. (1988). Culture and weight consciousness. *Journal of Psychosomatic Research, 32*, 573–577.

Pyle, R. L., Neuman, P. A., Halvorson, P. A., & Mitchell, J. E. (1991). Study of the prevalence of eating disorders in freshman college students. *International Journal of Eating Disorders, 10*, 667–677.

Sing Lee, M. B. (1996). Clinical lessons from the cross-cultural study of anorexia nervosa. *Eating Disorders Review, 7*, 1–4.

Thomas, V. G. (1989). Body-image satisfaction among black women. *Journal of Social Psychology, 129*, 107–112.

Vandereycken, W., & Van Deth, R. (1994). *From fasting saints to anorexic girls.* New York: New York University Press.

Wiseman, C. V., Gray, J. J., Mosimann, J. E., & Ahrens, A. H. (1992). Cultural expectations of thinness in women: An update. *International Journal of Eating Disorders, 11*, 85–89.

two

What Is an Eating Disorder?

ANOREXIA NERVOSA

Features of the Disorder The formal psychiatric name for this illness is anorexia nervosa, but it is often shortened to simply "anorexia." Anorexia nervosa should not be confused with general
anorexia, which means loss of appetite. People who have anorexia nervosa do not lose their appetites; rather, they refuse to
maintain a normal body weight. They lose at least 15 percent of
normal weight for height and have an intense fear of gaining
it back or becoming obese. They often weigh themselves several
times a day for fear of gaining weight and/or to see if they are
continuing to lose. Anorexics also have a highly unrealistic view
of their bodies, most often believing that they are fat even when
they are severely emaciated. Their self-esteem and self-worth are
based on size, weight, and body shape. Many anorexics wear
baggy clothes to hide their bodies, while others wear revealing
clothes to show off their underweight condition. Females stop
having menstrual cycles after a certain amount of weight is lost
or, in prepubescent girls, the menstrual cycle may not begin because of weight loss. Occasionally the period ceases some weeks

or months before the onset of weight loss, thus highlighting the psychological origins of the illness.

As the disease progresses, strange behaviors evolve relative to food and eating. The anorexic will often cut her food into tiny pieces, measuring and weighing everything she eats or drinks. She is likely to keep careful calorie and fat counts of every morsel of food she ingests. She may perform certain rituals, such as using particular plates or utensils or arranging her food items in lines or patterns. Even when she is at an unhealthy weight, the anorexic may exercise excessively and compulsively, insisting that she feels fine. Although she will deny hunger, her hunger pangs will become intense. She may be obsessed with reading and collecting recipes and may enjoy preparing food for others, but will not touch a bite herself. She may eat only when alone, for the presence of others at this time may feel like an intrusion.

Some anorexics start a pattern of binge eating followed by purging behavior to eliminate the calories they consume. Binge eating refers to eating a large amount of food in a relatively short period of time. The anorexic who binges feels out of control, as if she cannot stop herself, then feels tremendous anxiety over all she has eaten. Other negative feelings too, such as shame and guilt, cause her to use some means to get rid of the calories she has ingested. The most frequent form of purging is self-induced vomiting. Other means include laxatives, diuretics (fluid pills), enemas, and syrup of ipecac (a substance that induces vomiting). Some anorexics may use nonpurging methods such as fasting or excessive exercise. Studies have shown that anorexics who binge and purge are at greater risk for substance abuse than those who do not.

Personality changes, often observed along with physical changes, may include angry outbursts, isolative behavior, and depression. The depression may be secondary to the eating disorder, or it may be a primary problem. Anxiety, too, can be a primary problem or may be related to fears about food, body shape, and weight. It may also result from stressful or anxiety-provoking life circumstances. Anxiety disorders are quite common in anorexics and frequently occur before the eating disorder develops. Two studies showed that 60 percent and 83 percent, respectively, had an anxiety disorder at some point in their lives. Obsessive-compulsive traits can also be present, and may or may not be directly related to the anorexia. Obsessions are unwanted thoughts that repeatedly enter a person's mind and cause anxiety; compulsions are the behaviors that a person feels driven to do in order to decrease the anxiety caused by the obsessions. Examples of obsessive-compulsive behavior that are directly related to anorexia include constant calculation of calories and fat grams, frequent weighing, and compulsive exercising. Examples not directly related to an eating disorder may be frequent hand washing for fear of germ contamination, or checking repeatedly to confirm that appliances are turned off and doors are locked. At times, obsessive-compulsive behavior may be severe enough to warrant a diagnosis of obsessive-compulsive disorder and require treatment specifically designed for that disorder.

In addition to the emotional features already mentioned, the anorexic is likely to become irritable, indecisive, and defiant as she becomes entrenched in her illness. Typically, she withdraws from friends as her symptoms increase, and family quarrels over food and other issues intensify as her condition worsens. Sometimes family and friends feel she has become "another person," someone they no longer know. Her social withdrawal causes serious peer relationship problems, and her increasing physical debilitation creates panic, anxiety, and chaos within the family. The despair, isolation, and hopelessness of anorexia may even result in suicide. Observation of any combination of the warn-

WARNING SIGNS OF ANOREXIA

- Obsessive dieting
- Loss of menstrual cycle
- Claiming to feel fat when obviously not overweight
- Measuring self-worth in terms of weight and shape
- Preoccupation with food, calories, and nutrition
- Preparing food for others but not for self
- Hiding and collecting food
- Denial of hunger
- Excessive exercising
- Frequent weighing
- Use of laxatives and/or diuretics
- Vomiting to get rid of food eaten
- Strange behaviors relative to food and eating
- Exercise immediately preceding or following eating
- Complaints of feeling bloated or nauseated when eating normal or small amounts of food
- Attempts to get diet instructions and/or diet pills from doctors
- Fear of being unable to stop eating
- Isolation from peers and family
- Wearing bulky clothing to hide figure
- Sleep difficulties

ing signs and symptoms of anorexia should cause concern and provoke investigation into a potential problem.

Medical Complications Anorexia is a life-threatening condition that must be taken seriously, as it has one of the highest mortality rates of any psychiatric disorder. The death rate increases with the length of illness, and is as high as 20 percent for those who have been followed for twenty years. Anorexics often suffer from organ failure, as the body can no longer withstand the stress of starvation. For anorexics who use laxatives and/or diuretics to purge, important body chemicals such as potassium are frequently lost. This deficit can result in irregular heartbeats or even death from cardiac arrest or kidney failure. Chronic abuse of laxatives adversely affects the gastrointestinal system. The syrup of ipecac that some anorexics take to induce vomiting can cause a variety of heart problems as well as gastrointestinal and neuromuscular difficulties. Finally, a number of diet pills and so-called diet aids (for example, herbal supplements with the stimulant "ma huang," or ephedrine) are used for weight loss. As with laxatives and diuretics, anorexics will often abuse diet pills or diet supplements by taking more than the recommended dosage and taking them more frequently than suggested. These products can be quite dangerous; it is a mistake to believe that the diet products marketed as "all natural" and sold in health-food stores are safe. In truth, these products often contain ingredients that can produce potentially lethal side effects. In fact, deaths related to these products have been documented by the Food and Drug Administration. Identification of any such risky behavior constitutes cause for serious concern and immediate intervention.

The weight loss seen in anorexic patients is an obvious and invariable complication. The body reacts to starvation by slowing down to preserve calories for continued functioning of the heart and brain. Specific symptoms include a slower heart rate and lowered blood pressure, as well as hormonal disturbances. Reduced body fat leads to lowered body temperature and intolerance for cold. Prolonged starvation and malnutrition can also cause irregular heartbeats, heart failure, and cardiac arrest. The major medical complications of anorexia affect the brain, the

PHYSICAL SIGNS AND SYMPTOMS OF ANOREXIA

- Slow heart rate
- Low blood pressure
- Low body temperature
- Hair loss
- Dry and yellowed skin
- Brittle nails
- Lanugo (thin coating of soft body hair)
- Loss of menstrual cycle
- Early morning awakening
- Intolerance of cold
- Abdominal pain
- Weakness
- Swollen joints
- Lightheadedness
- Hyperactivity
- Constipation
- Fatigue

heart and circulatory system, the blood, the kidneys, the stomach and intestines, and the body's overall metabolism.

Amenorrhea (loss of three consecutive menstrual cycles) is a characteristic of anorexia in females that may precipitate additional medical complications. The menstrual cycle is a complicated system, and the exact cause of amenorrhea remains unclear. It is known, however, that abnormally low body fat content in addition to other biochemical disturbances contributes to the condition. While the dangers of amenorrhea may not be readily apparent, the consequences can be severe. Loss of bone mineral density can occur, which places girls and women at risk for osteopenia and osteoporosis. Various types of bone fractures may ultimately result. Current evidence suggests that these medical complications may persist even after the anorexic has restored her weight to normal. In terms of reproductive function, women who have a lifetime history of anorexia have been found to be at increased risk of obstetric complications, with the risk of miscarriage twice as great as for women with no history of anorexia. Furthermore, women who have been anorexic for a long period with chronic amenorrhea may compromise their reproductive function to the point of infertility.

Course of the Disorder Progress of anorexia over time varies greatly. Some anorexics recover fully after one episode of the illness; others return intermittently to a normal weight and then relapse. Unfortunately, some anorexics display a chronic course of symptoms that worsen over the span of many years, often ending in death. Females with anorexia are twelve times more likely to die than females the same age who have not had anorexia. Death most frequently results from the physical complications of starvation, electrolyte imbalance, or suicide. Chapter 5 gives relevant information and statistics.

BULIMIA NERVOSA

Features of the Disorder Although the formal diagnostic name for this illness is bulimia nervosa, it is better known by the public as bulimia. The disorder is characterized by binge eating, followed by eliminating the calories consumed in compensation for the binge. The bulimic usually either self-induces vomiting or takes laxatives or diuretics in an effort to eliminate the calories. She may diet strictly or fast between eating episodes to undo the damage, or she may exercise excessively in order to prevent weight gain. When binge eating, she feels out of control and believes she cannot stop. To meet the criteria for formal diagnosis, her binges occur at least twice a week over a three-month period, and she is persistently overconcerned with her body size, shape, and weight. This focus on the body strongly influences her negative self-image.

In spite of repeated binge eating, bulimics often manage to stay within five to ten pounds of normal weight. The typical bulimic is a professional dieter who often gains back the weight she loses and repeatedly feels like a failure. Her interest in her body and dieting becomes an obsession and she will often swing between strict dieting and periods of overeating. At some point in the process, she starts to feel great anxiety and may experience something akin to a "high" by ingesting large amounts of food. Like a drug, the food becomes a calming or numbing substance when anxiety and painful feelings about herself mount. Because of her overconcern with her body and her strong desire to be thin, the bulimic feels that she must get rid of the food and perhaps punish herself for what she considers to have been "bad" behavior. In an attempt to accomplish this task, she turns to purging or excessive exercise, usually within thirty minutes to an hour after the binge. Vomiting is typically induced by putting her fingers down her throat, although some individuals utilize foreign objects (spoons, forks, toothbrushes). These objects can be dangerous in and of themselves. Those who abuse laxatives usually take an excessive number to induce severe diarrhea after a binge and may increase the dosage over time.

As in anorexia, personality changes and emotional conditions are associated with bulimia. Depression is very common. Some of the depressive symptoms are directly related to binge/purge behaviors, along with the shame, guilt, and embarrassment associated with these practices. Much of the time, though, the depression that occurs is separate from bulimic behavior and has more to do with how the bulimic feels about herself, her family, and her life in general. Anxiety, almost always present, has been shown to play a major role in maintenance of the binge-purge cycle. The soothing and self-nurturing feelings that initially accompany the binge are quickly replaced by extreme concern over the calories consumed and fear of weight gain. In turn, the behaviors that are used to get rid of the calories reduce this anxiety and the cycle continues.

As with anorexics, anxiety disorders in bulimics are often present before the eating disorder develops. As the illness continues, those closest to the bulimic may notice her increased withdrawal and isolation from others, as well as her negative feelings about herself. She may never eat around others for fear of losing control or of being discovered. Greater difficulty with impulse control may be evident; some bulimics engage in stealing, risky sexual behavior, and drug or alcohol abuse. This acting-out may perpetuate a cycle of low self-esteem, depression, and self-destructive behavior, which creates further personality changes that are often of a rebellious nature.

People who have these periodic binges followed by purging, fasting, and/or exercise are aware that their relationship with food is abnormal and out of control. At first the behaviors to get rid of the calories may feel like the perfect answer to a dieter's dilemma. As the food intake increases and control is lost, however, bulimia becomes a nightmare for its victims. They are usually quite private and ritualistic because of the secretive and remorseful nature of the disorder. Even though the physical problems associated with the disease may become severe, the bulimic may still be reluctant to tell her physician what she is doing to her body. A great number of individuals are burdened with the illness for many years before telling a single person.

When friends and/or family become aware of the binge-eating and purging, it is usually because they notice large amounts of food missing or recognize signs of purging in the bathroom.

When first confronted, most bulimics deny the problem. They often become angry or hostile and may feel intruded upon when someone dares to enter their secret world. Yet somewhere inside, they may wish to be discovered so that something can be done to stop the despised and seemingly never-ending cycle.

As the illness progresses, binge-eating episodes become more frequent and the amount of food consumed during a binge increases. Relationships, work, school performance, and self-esteem often suffer dramatically. The depression associated with bulimia can be severe; unfortunately, suicide is sometimes viewed as the only solution. It is imperative that bulimics receive prompt professional attention once the disorder is discovered.

Medical Complications In normal-weight bulimics, most of the medical complications of starvation seen in anorexics are not present. However, the same serious problems related to purging that were described in individuals with anorexia (the loss of important body fluids and minerals) occur in persons with bulimia. We do not know what percentage of bulimics die from complications of the illness, but we do know that many deaths have been reported and that most bulimics have an assortment of medical problems associated with the disease.

Common complications, though certainly not the most serious, are dental and throat problems. It is not unusual for the bulimic's dentist to be the first to suspect her illness. Cavities, enamel erosion, persistent throat irritation, and chronic hoarseness can be the result of frequent vomiting. Abdominal pain, heartburn, and/or stomach cramps are frequent complaints, usually associated with overeating or purging behavior. Often bulimics will have swollen glands at the angle of the jaw, a result of bingeing and purging. Swelling or bloating over the stomach or abdominal area and in the extremities (fingers and toes)

WARNING SIGNS OF BULIMIA

- Obsessive dieting followed by binge eating
- Overconcern with body size, shape, and weight
- Rapid fluctuations in weight
- Frequent weighing
- Overeating associated with stress and/or anxiety
- Trips to the bathroom right after eating
- Guilt about eating
- Secretive eating
- Measuring self-worth in terms of body size, shape, and weight
- Disappearance of large quantities of food
- Hiding and collecting food
- Excessive exercise, particularly just before or after eating
- Swollen glands beneath the jaw
- Stealing, especially of food items
- Evidence of vomiting or laxative-induced diarrhea
- Abdominal pain
- Constipation
- Use of laxatives, diuretics, and/or diet pills

is caused by the fluid imbalance created by purging. Frequent menstrual irregularities are also seen, and sometimes bulimics lose their cycles altogether. The menstrual problems are usually due to excessive exercise and/or low body fat content. Dehydration, dryness of the skin, or a fine rash can result when too much body fluid is eliminated. Sometimes calluses or scars occur over the knuckles of the hand used to purge, from chronic abrasion by the teeth when the fingers are forced down the throat re-

PHYSICAL SIGNS AND SYMPTOMS OF BULIMIA

- Abdominal pain, bloating, and/or stomach cramps
- Heartburn
- Dental problems
- Persistent throat irritation
- Chronic hoarseness
- Swollen glands beneath the jaw
- Swelling or bloating of the extremities
- Menstrual irregularities
- Dry skin
- Dehydration
- Dry, brittle hair
- Callus or scar formation over knuckles
- Weakness and/or dizziness
- Broken blood vessels in the eyes
- Frequent weight fluctuations
- Diarrhea
- Constipation
- Fatigue

peatedly to induce vomiting. The most serious, life-threatening consequences of bulimia are esophageal tears, stomach rupture, kidney failure, heart failure, and cardiac arrest.

Course of the Disorder Not much is known about the course of untreated bulimia. According to clinic samples, however, disturbed eating is likely to persist for at least several years. Some individuals may have periods of spontaneous improvement and then relapse. Others follow a more chronic course, in which the symptoms worsen over time. Community samples have reported modest levels of spontaneous improvement.

EATING DISORDER NOT OTHERWISE SPECIFIED

When an individual presents with symptoms of an eating disorder but does not have all the specific symptoms of either anorexia or bulimia, a diagnosis of "Eating Disorder Not Otherwise Specified" is made. Common examples include someone who has all the symptoms of anorexia nervosa but is not yet 15 percent below normal body weight or who has not yet missed her period for three consecutive cycles, or a person who does not binge and/or purge as often as stipulated to meet the psychiatric definition of bulimia nervosa.

Even though these individuals do not meet the formal diagnostic criteria, their disorders must be taken seriously. The psychological changes and disturbances associated with anorexia or bulimia are likely to be present in one form or another. In addition, the medical complications seen in anorexia and bulimia apply to these persons, depending on which symptoms are present. For example, someone who has not yet dropped 15 percent below normal weight but has quickly lost weight may suffer from medical problems associated with rapid weight loss. Finally, it is likely that an individual with these symptoms will progress into more severe eating disordered behavior if prompt professional intervention is not sought. Much of the information presented regarding the development and treatment of anorexia and bulimia applies to those with an unspecified eating disorder. The issues involved in the development of the eating disorders are similar, whereas treatment will vary depending on the type of eating disordered behavior involved.

BINGE EATING DISORDER

Binge eating disorder will not be discussed in detail, as it is beyond the scope of this text to fully address the disorder and the typical coexisting problem of obesity (i.e., biological and genetic factors, medical complications, treatment). Instead, we offer a brief overview to familiarize readers with the illness. For more information on this particular disorder, see the supplemental readings in Appendix B.

Binge eating disorder, described as compulsive overeating in the past, is now recognized by the psychiatric community as a distinct problem. It consists of binge eating as seen in bulimia, but without the regular use of compensatory behaviors (purging, fasting, exercising) to get rid of the calories consumed during the binge. People who have this disorder feel out of control of their eating behavior and typically feel shame, guilt, depression, and/or embarrassment after bingeing. They often binge in secret, eat more rapidly than normal, and do not stop until they are uncomfortably full or are interrupted in some way. Their binges may last an entire day and continue over subsequent days. Studies have shown that people with this disorder eat more between binges than do people of the same weight who have no binge-eating problems. They also have great difficulty limiting their overall caloric intake, even though they have harsh personal standards for dieting. Unlike bulimics, those with this disorder report binges before engaging in any dieting behavior.

Obesity is common, and the medical complications that accompany it are often seen in binge eating disorder. It has been estimated that 30 percent of people seeking help for weight loss at university-based weight loss centers suffer from this disorder, and that about 8 percent of obese individuals in the community suffer from it, as well. Women are more frequently affected by binge eating disorder than are men, but not to the degree that we see in anorexia or bulimia. According to recent studies, women with this disorder outnumber men by a ratio of about three to two.

As with anorexia and bulimia, emotional changes are frequently seen. Most prominent is depression, which is often quite significant. During episodes of depression, individuals with this illness are particularly likely to gain weight as a result of severe bingeing. The depression may lead to a vicious cycle in which the person eats to relieve the feelings of depression, consequently gains weight, and then becomes even more depressed.

Much remains unknown about binge eating disorder because of its relatively new status as a distinct eating disorder. We do know, however, that it is treatable. The goals of treatment include normalization of eating (no bingeing, more control over eating behavior) and amelioration of accompanying psychological symptoms such as depression. The types of treatment described in later chapters for bulimia are, with certain modifications, applicable to binge eating disorder. Obese patients with binge eating disorder are likely to request assistance with weight loss. This type of treatment is often attempted after normalization of eating is accomplished. Dieting has not been shown to worsen binge eating in this group.

Selected Bibliography

Agras, W. S. (1987). *Eating disorders: Management of obesity, bulimia, and anorexia nervosa*. New York: Pergamon Press.

American Psychiatric Association. (1994). *Diagnostic and statistical manual of mental disorders* (4th ed.). Washington, D.C.: Author.

American Psychiatric Association Work Group on Eating Disorders. (2000). Practice guideline for the treatment of patients with eating disorders (Rev.). *American Journal of Psychiatry, 157 (Suppl. 1)*, 1–39.

Bulik, C. M., Sullivan, P. F., Fear, J. L., & Joyce, P. R. (1997). Eating disorders and antecedent anxiety disorders: A controlled study. *Acta Psychiatra Scandinavica, 96*, 101–107.

Bulik, C. M., Sullivan, P. F., Fear, J. L., Pickering, A., Dawn, A., & McCullin, M. (1999). Fertility and reproduction in women with anorexia nervosa: A controlled study. *Journal of Clinical Psychiatry, 60,* 130–135.

Bulik, C. M., Wade, T. D., & Kendler, K. S. (2001). Characteristics of monozygotic twins discordant for bulimia nervosa. *International Journal of Eating Disorders, 29,* 1–10.

Food and Drug Administration. (2000). *Dietary supplements containing ephedrine alkaloids; Withdrawal in part* (DHHS Publ. No. 65–FR 17510). Washington, D.C.: U.S. Government Printing Office.

Godart, N. T., Flament, M. F., Lecrubier, Y., & Jeammet, P. (2000). Anxiety disorders in anorexia nervosa and bulimia nervosa: Comorbidity and chronology of appearance. *European Psychiatry, 15,* 38–45.

Goldbloom, D. S. (1993). Menstrual and reproductive function in the eating disorders. In A. S. Kaplan & P. E. Garfinkel (Eds.), *Medical issues and the eating disorders: The interface* (pp. 165–175). New York: Brunner/Mazel.

Gross, J., & Rosen, J. C. (1988). Bulimia in adolescents: Prevalence and psychological correlates. *International Journal of Eating Disorders, 7,* 51–61.

Harris, E. C., & Barraclough, B. (1998). Excess mortality of mental disorder. *British Journal of Psychiatry, 173,* 11–53.

Hawkins, R. C., & Clement, P. F. (1980). Development and construct validation of a self-report measure of binge eating tendencies. *Addictive Behaviors, 5,* 219–226.

Leon, G. R., Carroll, K., Chernyk, K. B., & Finn, S. (1985). Binge eating and associated habit patterns with college student and identified bulimic populations. *International Journal of Eating Disorders, 4,* 43–57.

Marcus, M. D. (1995). Binge eating and obesity. In K. D. Brownell & C. G. Fairburn (Eds.), *Eating disorders and obesity: A comprehensive handbook* (pp. 441–444). New York: Guilford Press.

Marcus, M. D. (1997). Adapting treatment for patients with binge-eating disorder. In D. M. Garner & P. E. Garfinkel (Eds.), *Handbook of treatment for eating disorders* (2nd ed., pp. 484–493). New York: Guilford Press.

Mitchell, J. E. (1995). New directions in the diagnosis and treatment of eating disorders. In R. Pies (Ed.), *Advances in psychiatric medicine* (Suppl. to *Psychiatric Times*).

Prather, R. C., & Williamson, D. A. (1988). Psychopathology associated with bulimia, binge eating, and obesity. *International Journal of Eating Disorders, 4,* 177–184.

Siemers, B., Chakmakjian, Z., & Gench, B. (1996). Bone density patterns in women with anorexia nervosa. *International Journal of Eating Disorders, 19,* 179–186.

Sullivan, P. F. (1995). Mortality in anorexia nervosa. *American Journal of Psychiatry, 152,* 1073–1074.

Swift, W. J., Andrews, D., & Barklage, N. E. (1986). The relationship between affective disorders and eating disorders: A review of the literature. *American Journal of Psychiatry, 143,* 290–299.

Theander, S. (1985). Outcome and prognosis in anorexia nervosa and bulimia: Some results of previous investigations compared with those of a Swedish long term study. *Journal of Psychiatric Research, 19,* 493–508.

Tolstoi, L. G. (1990). Ipecac-induced toxicity in eating disorders. *International Journal of Eating Disorders, 9,* 371–375.

Weiss, S. W., & Ebert, M. H. (1983). Psychological and behavioral characteristics of normal weight bulimics and normal weight controls. *Psychosomatic Medicine, 45,* 293–303.

Willard, S. G. (1990). *Anorexia and bulimia: The potential devastation of dieting.* Plainfield, New Jersey: Patient Education Press.

Willard, S. G., Winstead, D. K., Anding, R., & Dudley, P. (1989). Laxative detoxification in bulimia nervosa. In W. Johnson (Ed.), *Advances in eating disorders,* Vol. 2 (pp. 219–236). Greenwich, Connecticut: JAI Press.

Wolf, E. M., & Crowther, J. H. (1983). Personality and eating habit variables as predictors of severity of binge eating and weight. *Addictive Behaviors, 8,* 335–344.

Yager, J., Landsverk, J., & Edelstein, C. K. (1987). A 20-month follow-up study of 628 women with eating disorders, I: Course and severity. *American Journal of Psychiatry, 144,* 1172–1177.

Zwaan, M., & Mitchell, J. E. (1993). Medical complications of anorexia nervosa and bulimia nervosa. In A. S. Kaplan & P. E. Garfinkel (Eds.), *Medical issues and the eating disorders: The interface* (pp. 60–100). New York: Brunner/Mazel.

three

Who Is Likely to Develop an Eating Disorder?

More than 90 percent of individuals with eating disorders are female. The prevalence of *diagnosable* eating disorders in males is estimated to be at a ratio of one male case for every ten female cases. Some researchers believe that the numbers are closer to one male for every six females. In cases of anorexia occurring before puberty, boys constitute approximately 20–25 percent of diagnosed cases. Thus, the gender gap in terms of prevalence is not as large among boys and girls as it is later in adolescence and young adulthood.

Eating disorders tend to strike during the adolescent years, with an estimated 85 percent of cases beginning during this time. Health care professionals are seeing these illnesses more often than ever before in young adolescents and preteens. In fact, eating disorders are the third most common chronic illnesses in adolescent girls. Although there is debate over the prevalence rates of eating disorders in female adolescents, somewhere between 0.5 and 5.0 percent of them will develop anorexia, and a higher percentage will develop bulimia. The American Psychiatric Association reports that the two age ranges when the likelihood of developing anorexia increases are around fourteen and eighteen years. For bulimia, the average age of onset is approximately eighteen. The majority of people we have seen with anorexia or bulimia in our own clinical practices developed the disorder somewhere between the ages of twelve and twenty-five. This does not mean, however, that anyone younger or older is immune from these disorders. We have treated children as young as eight years of age and women up to age sixty-eight. Sadly, children as young as five years worry about their body image and are afraid of becoming fat. One study has shown that girls are beginning to diet as early as age eight. These facts make a frightening statement about the emphasis our society places on female appearance. It is also alarming that children in the throes of emotional and physical development may be short-changed medically and developmentally by these illnesses (for details, see Chapters 2 and 4).

It was traditionally believed that Caucasian women were at higher risk for developing eating disorders than were minority women. One review of studies conducted with American female minorities has contradicted this belief by showing that Hispanic females are as often affected by eating disorders as Caucasian females. The review also found that Asian Americans and African Americans are less likely to develop eating disorders than their Caucasian counterparts. Other studies have shown that African American women are more likely to develop bulimia than they are to develop anorexia, and that they are more prone to cyclical binge eating than are Caucasian females. Even so, eating disorders are considered to be more related to culture than to race. As an example, the increased incidence of eating disorders in Japan is believed to be a result of Japan's relatively recent adoption of more Westernized ideals of beauty, coupled with more nontraditional views of the roles of women in Japanese society. These changes are thought to produce anxiety and stress in Japanese girls, as their roles in society involve more choices and ambiguity than ever before. Another example involves African American girls and women. In general, the African American culture values a larger female body ideal than the Caucasian culture. As an African American girl or woman assimilates more into traditional Caucasian culture, however, her risk of developing an eating disorder increases. Thus, it seems that cultural values of beauty and cultural views of the roles of women in society are crucial factors in determining susceptibility to the development of eating disorders. We will have more to say on the societal influences on eating disorders, as well as the common personality characteristics seen in eating disordered individuals, in Chapter 4.

The majority of girls and women with eating disorders who come to the attention of treatment providers are apt to be very intelligent and relatively well educated. They also tend to come from middle-class to upper-class families. While eating disorders are becoming more widespread and individuals from a variety of backgrounds are being affected, it appears that ethnic-minority females are less likely to seek treatment than Caucasian females. Some researchers believe that this phenomenon is due to a combination of factors that might include financial problems, inadequate health insurance, fear of being labeled, negative beliefs about treatment, and lack of knowledge about treatment resources. In sum, very little is currently understood about the prevalence, development, and treatment response of ethnic-minority females with eating disorders. These important topics warrant further investigation.

Research has shown that competitive female athletes are at greater risk for the development of eating disorders than are females of the same age in the general population. Furthermore, female athletes appear to be at greater risk for developing eating disordered attitudes and behaviors than are male athletes. In particular, females who engage in sports that value thinness —ballet, gymnastics, figure skating, distance running—are at greater risk. Along with the general factors that contribute to the development of an eating disorder, athletes have sports-related beliefs and pressures that make them more vulnerable as well. Many athletes, for example, erroneously believe that being thinner and having extremely low body fat will improve their performance. Parents, coaches, and other athletes may actually encourage the beliefs, attitudes, and behaviors that often lead to these illnesses. Similarly, women in occupations that emphasize thinness and appearance, such as models and ballerinas, are at greater risk for developing an eating disorder. Military women, too, have been identified as more vulnerable to eating disorders for some of the same reasons as civilian female athletes, including the societal pressures for thinness as well as pressures related to military performance. (See Chapter 7 for sports and occupational factors related to males with eating disorders. For more detailed information on athletes and eating disorders, see Appendix B.)

Research has demonstrated that adolescents and young women with chronic diseases that require strict dietary regimens, such as diabetes and phenylketonuria (PKU), are at risk for the development of eating disorders. Eating disorders may also develop secondary to other chronic illnesses such as cystic fibrosis, inflammatory bowel disease, Crohn's disease, hypothyroidism, and hyperthyroidism. In all cases, the person with the eating disorder may engage in medically dangerous behaviors by misusing treatment of the medical disease to facilitate weight loss or purging. An example is the diabetic patient's omission of insulin for purposes of weight loss.

Selected Bibliography

Akan, G. E., & Grilo, C. M. (1995). Sociocultural influences on eating attitudes and behaviors, body image, and psychological functioning: A comparison of African American, Asian American, and Caucasian college women. *International Journal of Eating Disorders, 18*, 180–187.

American Dietetic Association. (2001). Position of the American Dietetic Association: Nutrition intervention in the treatment of anorexia nervosa, bulimia nervosa, and eating disorders not otherwise specified (EDNOS). *Journal of the American Dietetic Association, 101*, 810–819.

American Psychiatric Association. (1994). *Diagnostic and statistical manual of mental disorders* (4th ed., Rev.). Washington, D.C.: Author.

American Psychiatric Association Work Group on Eating Disorders. (2000). Practice guideline for the treatment of patients with eating disorders (Rev.). *American Journal of Psychiatry, 157 (Suppl. 1)*, 1–39.

Andersen, A. E. (1990). *Males with eating disorders.* New York: Brunner/Mazel.

Antisdel, J. E., & Chrisler, J. C. (2000). Comparison of eating attitudes and behaviors among adolescent and young women with type 1 diabetes mellitus and phenylketonuria. *Journal of Developmental and Behavioral Pediatrics, 21*, 81–86.

Crago, M., Shisslak, C. M., & Estes, L. S. (1996). Eating disturbances among African American minority groups: A review. *International Journal of Eating Disorders, 19*, 239–248.

Fairburn, C. G., & Cooper, P. J. (1982). Self-induced vomiting and bulimia nervosa: An undetected problem. *British Medical Journal, 284*, 1153-1155.

Fairburn, C. G., & Cooper, P. J. (1984). The clinical features of bulimia nervosa. *British Journal of Psychiatry, 144*, 238–246.

Feldman, W., Feldman, E., & Goodman, J. T. (1988). Culture versus biology: Children's attitudes toward thinness and fatness. *Pediatrics, 81*, 190–194.

Goldman, E. L. (1996). Eating disorders on the rise in preteens, adolescents. *Clinical Psychiatry News, 24*, 10.

Johnson, C., Powers, P. S., & Dick, R. (1999). Athletes and eating disorders: The National Collegiate Athletic Association study. *International Journal of Eating Disorders, 26,* 179–188.

Lauder, T. D., Williams, M. V., Campbell, C. S., Davis, G. D., & Sherman, R. A. (1999). Abnormal eating behaviors in military women. *Medicine and Science in Sports and Exercise, 31,* 1265–1271.

Nasser, M. (1988). Culture and weight consciousness. *Journal of Psychosomatic Research, 32,* 573–577.

Nasser, M. (1998). Eating disorders: Between cultural specificity and globalization. *Eating Disorders Review, 9,* 1–3.

Powers, P. S. (1997). Management of patients with comorbid medical conditions. In D. M. Garner & P. E. Garfinkel (Eds.), *Handbook of treatment for eating disorders* (2nd ed., pp. 424–436). New York: Guilford Press.

Pumariega, A. J., Gustavson, C. R., & Gustavson, J. C. (1994). Eating attitudes in African-American women: The essence. *Eating Disorders: Journal of Treatment and Prevention, 2,* 5–16.

Pyle, R. L., Mitchell, J. E., & Eckert, E. D. (1981). Bulimia: A report of 34 cases. *Journal of Clinical Psychiatry, 42,* 60–64.

Rucker, C. E., & Cash, T. F. (1992). Body image, body size perceptions and eating behaviors among African-American and White college women. *International Journal of Eating Disorders, 3,* 291–299.

Shapiro, S., Newcomb, M., & Loeb, T. B. (1997). Fear of fat, disregulated-restrained eating, and body-esteem: Prevalence and gender differences among eight- to ten-year-old children. *Journal of Clinical Child Psychology, 26,* 358–365.

Shmolling, P. (1988). Eating Attitudes Test scores in relation to weight, socioeconomic status, and family stability. *Psychological Reports, 63,* 295–298.

Smith, J. E., & Krejci, J. (1991). Minorities join the majority: Eating disturbances among Hispanic and Native American youth. *International Journal of Eating Disorders, 10,* 179–186.

Striegal-Moore, R. H. (2001). In M. K. Stein (ed.), Exploring better access to care for minority, underserved populations. *Eating Disorders Review, 12,* 1–4.

Striegal-Moore, R. H., Wilfley, D. E., Pike, K. M., Dohm, F. A., & Fairburn, C. G. (2000). Recurrent binge eating in black American women. Archives of Family Medicine, 9, 83 87.

Willard, S. G., & Maresh, R. D. (1996). Anorexia nervosa in an African American female of a lower socioeconomic background. *European Eating Disorders Review, 4,* 95–99.

four

Why Does Someone Develop an Eating Disorder?

No one knows exactly how or why an eating disorder occurs. We do know that there is no single reason for someone to develop one of these illnesses, and we know that eating disorders are not about food. The thoughts and behaviors having to do with eating, weight, and body image are symptoms of deeper psychological conflicts and issues that drive the eating disordered behavior. Just as fever signals some sort of infection that a person's body is trying to fight, an eating disorder is indicative of other underlying problems. The fact that the principal concerns of eating disorders are not actually food, calories, and weight often confuses families and friends because food and weight related issues are the obvious focus of the eating disordered individual. For example, the anorexic will adamantly complain that she is fat and must restrict calories to lose more weight. The bulimic may claim that vomiting is the only way she can control her weight. Both often say that if it were not for problems with food and weight, they would be fine.

The eating disordered person is initially surprised by the notion that eating disorders are about issues other than eating and body shape. The focus on food and weight serves to prevent her from thinking about disturbing, underlying issues such as a history of physical or sexual abuse. The obsession with the eating disorder distracts her from unpleasant thoughts and emotions and actually helps her to feel better about herself. The specific ways that eating disorders enhance self-esteem vary, but feelings of increased control, confidence, and achievement are frequently reported. The disordered behaviors can also be a means of getting attention and feeling special.

THE BIOPSYCHOSOCIAL MODEL

We have said that there is never one single cause of eating disorders. Instead, they are quite complicated, and a variety of factors appear to contribute to their development. Many proposed explanations focus primarily on one aspect or another of eating disorders, whether biological, cultural, or psychological. These models are too simplistic or limited to account for all facets of these disorders. A "biopsychosocial" approach includes all dimensions of eating disorders and explains why some women develop these illnesses while others do not, despite commonality across certain variables. It also provides an effective model for treatment. The specific components of this comprehensive model include biological factors, societal influences, individual personality features, and family characteristics.

Biological Factors A great deal of the research examining biological factors that may make some young women more susceptible to eating disorders has focused on genetic components. In particular, researchers have compared the prevalence of anorexia in sets of identical and fraternal twins. Difficulties with this type of research include the small sample sizes, how patients are recruited for studies, differences in the definitions of anorexia, the extent to which twins share a similar environment, and similarities in social life (environmental factors). In any case, researchers who have reviewed studies with satisfactory designs report that there is evidence of a genetic predisposition to anorexia. Unknown, however, is the degree to which genetics influences the development of the disorder. What may actually be "inherited" are certain personality characteristics or traits that increase susceptibility to the development of an eating disorder. In particular, those with anxious, obsessional, and perfectionistic personality traits seem more vulnerable. Additionally, studies have shown that a high percentage of women with anorexia, up to 90 percent in one study, had an anxiety disorder before the onset of anorexia. This finding, again, suggests that excessive anxiety may be a risk factor for anorexia.

Another type of study that looks at genetic influences involves examining whether or not these disorders tend to run in families. When these family risk studies focus on anorexia, researchers find that the immediate relatives of anorexics are at greater risk of developing anorexia than are people in the general population, thereby supporting the idea that there is a biological vulnerability. Again, it is difficult to sort out the degree to which the biological predisposition affects the development of anorexia, as many environmental factors must also be taken into consideration.

Although binge eating is primarily psychologically motivated, a biological vulnerability may be due in part to the body's attempts to compensate for the effects of rigorous dieting and physiological food deprivation. More specifically, girls and women who starve themselves or chronically diet may be trying to maintain a weight below that which is natural and healthy for body frame and height. Those who attempt to maintain an unhealthy weight may experience biologically driven eating behavior (such as binge eating) that is aimed at increasing weight to the body's preferred status. This kind of biologically driven binge eating has been observed in other groups subjected to starvation or chronic food restriction, such as prisoners of war or laboratory subjects who did not have eating disorders.

With regard to biological factors that may predispose a woman to bulimia, some researchers have questioned whether or not the bulimic behaviors are related to depressive symptoms. Specifically, it has been speculated that bulimia is a symptom, or a behavioral expression, of biologically driven depression. For instance, family risk studies have shown a high incidence of depression among close relatives of bulimic women. In addition, biochemical evidence of depression has been found in bulimics at rates that are similar to those of individuals with depressive disorders, and with greater frequency than in the general population. There is also evidence, however, suggesting that the behavioral symptoms of bulimia occur before the depression and that the depression is secondary to the bulimia. Further, the reportedly high rates of depression in close relatives of both anorexics and bulimics occur primarily when the eating disordered patient also has a formal diagnosis of depression. When this significant level of depression is not present, the rates of depression in close relatives decrease. These findings, taken together, suggest that bulimia is a separate disorder from depression but that the two problems often occur together.

A recent genetic study of bulimia examined pairs of identical twins in which one twin met the criteria for bulimia and the other did not. Individuals in the first category were much more likely to report a lifetime history of generalized anxiety disorder, in which the person was almost constantly worried about a variety of life circumstances and potential problems. In 75 percent of the cases, the anxiety disorder either preceded the eating disorder or started simultaneously. Furthermore, the individual twins who met the criteria for bulimia were described by their mothers as anxious and fearful as children, whereas the twins who were not bulimic were not so described. The findings suggest that genetically based features of anxiety may be a risk factor for developing bulimia. This possibility is consistent with other studies that have shown anxiety disorders predating the development of eating disorders.

As with anorexia, family risk studies evaluating biological factors that may predispose a woman to the development of bulimia have shown that the immediate relatives of bulimics are more likely to develop bulimia. According to some researchers, the genetic evidence is equivocal because twin studies have been inconsistent in supporting a genetic link. Others argue that studies with more sophisticated and powerful designs provide strong evidence for genetic susceptibility to bulimia. Thus, the degree to which bulimia is inherited remains debatable.

Finally, chemical abnormalities in the brain such as serotonin dysregulation have been found in both anorexia and bulimia. It is not known whether these abnormalities are part of the cause, or are a result of the disorders.

Societal Influences We noted in Chapter 1 that there are numerous ways in which our society contributes to the obsession of girls and women with beauty, fitness, and—most important—thinness. Our culture has spawned an atmosphere in which females feel pressured to be successful by society's unrealistic standards to be "superwoman." Standards for success include being thin and beautiful, having husbands and children, and pursuing professions and careers that carry with them power and financial prowess. Confusion, anxiety, and concern about these role expectations, and ambivalence about one's position in society, are thought to be related to the increase in eating disorders seen in our culture and around the world. These disturbing feelings may propel some girls and women to look to their appearance as a way to feel in control. Today's greater sexual freedom for women is a phenomenon that produces even more anxiety and fear. The end result is a physical obsession of epidemic proportions, wherein up to 80 percent of teenage girls worry about being overweight and children as young as five years of age have body image concerns and fear becoming overweight. Unhealthy dieting is extremely common in girls and women who believe that losing weight and perfecting their bodies is the answer to life's problems.

As mentioned earlier, studies show an increasing prevalence of eating disorders in societies that identify with a more Western view of attractiveness. Cultures and societies that hold ideals of female beauty similar to those of Caucasian Americans in terms of the overvaluation of thinness and the goal of "perfection" are increasing the risk for eating disorders by encouraging women to attempt to attain these ideals. It is virtually impossible these days to browse through a magazine, read a newspaper, or watch television for any substantial period without seeing the promotion of diets, exercise programs, fitness centers, and/or dietary aids. This media hype has led to the popularity of dieting among young women and adolescent girls, with 75 percent of female teenagers dieting before the age of sixteen. Furthermore, the last two decades have seen an increase in the use of dietary aids such as diet pills, exercise equipment, and materials designed to teach people how to lose weight. The 1990s saw an explosion in the number of specific diets and diet books on the market. In fact, it was recently estimated that Americans spend about $40 billion per year in pursuit of thinness!

It should be obvious at this point that we are a culture preoccupied with body shape and weight, and that our values of beauty relate disproportionately to thinness. The real danger, however, lies in the fact that this overvaluation of beauty and thinness often leads to early and stringent dieting, which has been shown to be the most common factor leading to the development of eating disorders.

The media is a powerful influence perpetuating America's obsession with beauty and thinness. Modern television, magazines, and movies present women labeled "beautiful" or "attractive" as very thin. Consistent with this trend, the weight of beauty contestants has steadily decreased over the years, even when height is taken into consideration. One study found that the average weights of Miss America beauty contestants are 13–19 percent lower than expected for age. In popular women's magazines, the number of diet and exercise articles has significantly increased. In spite of these trends, census reports indicate that the average weight of a woman in the general population increased six pounds from the 1960s to the 1980s. Hence, the actual weight of the typical American female is becoming further removed from our society's ideal, suggesting that a woman has to lose even more weight to meet the cultural standard of thinness.

Women who actively attempt to meet the current ideal of thinness and do not take into consideration personal body frame and/or natural weight setpoint (that is, biologically favored weight), may find it not only psychologically frustrating to lose weight, but biologically difficult or impossible. The issue is further complicated by the finding that healthy Caucasian women are apt to overestimate their actual body size. This tendency is commonly referred to as distorted body image. Not surprisingly, it is almost always present in eating disordered individuals. Ironically, even if someone with an eating disorder attains what she deems to be the social ideal of thinness, she is unlikely to acknowledge that she is thin enough because of her distorted body image. In other words, she is likely to continue to see herself as fat, even after significant weight loss. With the popularity of plastic surgery, particularly liposuction, such misperceptions about the body are leading to pathological and repetitive requests for surgery that may represent a modified version of purging behavior.

In years past, young women felt pressured to look as attractive as possible in order to find a husband. Today they are feeling additional pressure to achieve professional success without sacrificing attractiveness or femininity. Thinness may therefore represent a modern means for women to attain power and success comparable to the achievements of men, while simultaneously holding on to society's expectations of beauty. Some women come to view food and weight as entities they can control when feeling they have little control over other societal demands. This idea fits with findings demonstrating that individuals with eating disorders have relatively high needs for control, yet actually believe they have relatively little say over what happens in their lives.

Individual Personality Characteristics and Emotional Features   Most girls and young women in our culture are subjected to societal pressures for thinness that may lead them to diet, but not all of them develop eating disorders. Along with societal pressures and biological factors that may contribute to the development of eating disorders, certain personality characteristics have been linked to women who develop these illnesses. Low self-esteem and perfectionism as well as the need for achievement, control, and approval are traits consistently seen in such individuals.

Anorexics tend to be quite anxious; they strive to please everyone around them and avoid any source of potential conflict. When young, anorexics tend to be "model children" who are always compliant and rarely display normal teenage rebellion. These characteristics ultimately prevent them from recognizing and honestly expressing their feelings. Fears of sexuality and a refusal to grow up are commonly seen. Arthur Crisp, an international expert on anorexia, has described it as "an abortion of development" and a "maturational crisis."

Bulimics may have any combination of the features listed above, though on average they tend to show more emotionality than those with anorexia. They are more likely, for instance, to experience intense emotions that are confusing to them, such as alternating among feelings of happiness, despair, and anger. Often they are not sure why they feel as they do. Bulimics are more likely to exhibit teenage rebellion seen in self-destructive behaviors such as alcohol or other drug abuse, sexual promiscuity, or shoplifting.

An important emotional feature that stems in part from the characteristics already mentioned is lack of identity. When an individual is unable to figure out what she feels, why she feels as she does, or how to have her emotional needs met in a healthy manner, it is difficult for her to form a sense of self. When she is busy living up to the expectations of others and trying to please those around her, she is prevented from discovering her own values and opinions as well as what she really desires for herself.

In addition to personality characteristics that may make someone vulnerable to the development of an eating disorder, disturbances in thought patterns play a role. Individuals with eating disorders tend to think in ways that distort information, often in a negative fashion. Among these patterns are illogical thinking, imagining the worst in situations, ignoring positive events or information, focusing on negative events and information, and dichotomous (all-or-none) thinking. Dichotomous thinking is when a person views things only in the extremes. An eating disordered individual frequently thinks in terms of being either "skinny or fat" and therefore "being a good person or a bad person." This erroneous thinking results in a variety of negative emotions that might include depression, anxiety, self-hate, anger, and/or guilt.

The personality traits and disturbed thinking patterns detailed above can inhibit formation of identity and result in inadequate or faulty coping skills, preventing young women from effectively dealing with life's stresses and problems. In addition, these characteristics often increase the vulnerability of young women to cultural pressures for thinness in their attempts to be perfect or at least to improve themselves. They may then turn to their bodies as an imagined means of coping with the problems in their lives and as a way to feel in control.

Family Characteristics There are women affected by societal pressures for thinness who diet and possess the personality characteristics listed above, but do not succumb to eating disorders. What, then, might be another ingredient that contributes to the development of an eating disorder?

Although no one knows for sure what role the family plays in this context, we do know that the family provides the backdrop against which eating disorders develop. For decades, clinicians have noted the association between eating disorders and difficulty with individuation and emotional separation from the family of origin. Individuation refers to a person's ability to establish a separate identity, including opinions, tastes, values, and goals that differ from those of the family of origin. In those who successfully complete this necessary developmental task, an overlap may remain among opinions, values, and goals, yet an independent and distinct sense of self emerges, which differs from that of the family. Family therapists have frequently described families who have a daughter with an eating disorder as enmeshed (emotionally overinvolved with fused identities), making separation difficult.

It is never useful or appropriate to blame any family member or members for the development of an eating disorder; these illnesses are complex and occur for a variety of reasons. However, as we know that the family represents the holding environment for the child, it is always important to look at which aspects of the family might relate to occurrence of the disease.

A great deal of information has been compiled on the characteristics of families of individuals with eating disorders. Subsequently, researchers have described several types of family systems frequently seen. These descriptions, however, are not definitive. Families may recognize qualities in themselves from more than one type of system, or from none.

One common system is the "perfect family," in which rigid rules consciously or unconsciously govern the behavior of all family members. The female with an eating disorder in this type of family tends to be a very high achiever by family standards. The family reputation is sacred; the members are expected to think, act, and feel the "right" way. Appearance is of utmost importance, as this family type needs to seem "perfect" to outside observers. An eating disorder in this family system may help the anorexic or bulimic to accomplish one or more of the following: (1) passive rebellion against the family system; (2) creation of a separate identity; (3) suppression of feelings by focusing on food; and (4) assertion of control over herself in the midst of a controlling family.

A second family type is the "overprotective family," characterized by its nurturance of dependence and refusal to acknowledge any need for independence. Anger and conflict are not well tolerated and are seldom overtly displayed. Since the adolescent period is fraught with change and conflict, many difficult issues are never openly or directly resolved. As a result, passive-aggressive behaviors develop, thereby hindering direct expressions of rebellion. Eating disorder symptoms in this family type may serve as a means of passively rebelling against the family and indirectly expressing anger, while simultaneously reaffirming dependence on the family members. In this way, the eating disordered family member does not risk direct anger, criticism, or rejection by the rest of the family because she is viewed as "sick." In addition, when children are overprotected and scrutinized, they sometimes become self-conscious and perfectionistic, fearing that an error will cause great dissatisfaction to the parents. The quest for perfection can cause low self-esteem as the child realizes that she cannot be perfect in every way all the time. Consequently, she is likely to experience feelings of inadequacy and failure. Some cases of overprotective parenting in families with an anorexic daughter have been linked to unresolved grief resulting from a previous obstetric loss such as a miscarriage or the death of a child. Often, the anorexic daughter is the next child born after the loss.

The third family type is the "chaotic family." In contrast to the perfect family, which has many rules, the chaotic family has virtually none. Organization and consistency are lacking, and the availability and expression of love are unpredictable. Conflict resolution is usually forced by physical aggression and/or psychological intimidation. An eating disorder within this family atmosphere may be a safe way for the afflicted individual to express anger, separate herself from the abusive situation, and/or assert consistency in her life. The illness can also, however, function as an extension of abuse against herself.

Certain other family characteristics are commonly found among families with an eating disordered child. Often another family member is either overweight or excessively thin. There may be an overconcern with food and food-related issues in the household. It is not unusual to see one or both parents involved with chronic dieting and/or rigid exercise regimens. Daughters of these families may be particularly susceptible to dieting and exercising as a means of bonding with parents who are obviously preoccupied with such matters themselves.

Some parents of children with eating disorders live their lives

peated attempts to stop the behaviors, and feel that their behavior is beyond their control. In addition, these individuals use the substances to cope with stress, may lie about their behavior, require more of the food or drug over time to get the desired effects, and attempt to keep their problem secret. The addiction model of eating disorders holds that affected persons are biologically vulnerable to the chemical effects of certain foods, such as sugar and white flour, that are "toxic" to their systems and result in physical addiction to these foods.

While this explanation offers a reason why the individual with an eating disorder feels compelled to do what she does and cannot stop, there is no support for this model other than the similarities already mentioned. Chemical dependency, or addiction, is characterized by the following features: physical tolerance of a substance, so that increased amounts of it are required to get the desired effect; physical dependence on the drug; physical withdrawal symptoms when the drug is stopped; biologically based craving for the drug; and loss of control over drug use that is biologically driven. There is no scientific evidence for any of these biological features in eating disorders. The loss of control seen in eating disorders is a perceived loss, not a biologically based loss. Those with bulimic symptoms do not always binge after eating an allegedly toxic food such as sugar, especially if they are not allowed to purge afterward. In addition, individuals who binge eat fear doing so because of likely weight gain and therefore have a strong urge to control their food intake. They use a great deal of self-restraint and self-denial in their attempts to avoid binges by restricting food consumption. No similar process occurs in the case of alcohol and other drug addictions.

These fundamental differences in the disorders lead to necessary differences in treatment. The nutritional goals in treating bulimic symptoms are to moderate dietary intake and loosen the self-imposed restraint over food. In the treatment of addictions, the goal is to impose or strengthen self-restraint by means of abstinence. Many groups of Overeaters Anonymous, a twelve-step organization that applies the addiction model to eating disorders, advocate abstinence from so-called toxic foods, rigid dietary practices, recognition that a person is powerless over the disorder, and all-or-nothing thinking (for instance, certain foods are "bad," relapse results if you eat a "bad" food). Unfortunately, this model actually perpetuates the psychological features and rigid dietary practices that play a major role in the development and maintenance of eating disorders. Moreover, it does not address the underlying psychological conflicts and psychosocial issues that are paramount. Finally, the addiction model argues that a person is never completely cured. Yet eating disorders research, and our clinical experience as well as that of others, shows that people can, in fact, fully recover from these illnesses.

Having said all of the above, we should note that there are aspects of the traditional twelve-step model and support groups that are thought by many to be beneficial. For more information, see Chapter 5.

Selected Bibliography

Agras, W. S. (1987). *Eating disorders: Management of obesity, bulimia, and anorexia nervosa*. New York: Pergamon Press.

Allerdissen, R., Florin, I., & Rost, W. (1981). Psychological characteristics of women with bulimia nervosa. *Behavior Analysis Modification, 4,* 314–317.

Bauer, B. G., Anderson, W. P., & Hyatt, R. W. (1986). *Bulimia: Book for therapist and client*. Muncie, Indiana: Accelerated Development.

Birtchnell, S. A., Lacey, J. H., & Harte, A. (1985). Body image distortion in bulimia nervosa. *British Journal of Psychiatry, 147,* 408–412.

Bruch, H. (1973). *Eating disorders: Obesity, anorexia nervosa, and the person within*. New York: Basic Books.

Bulik, C., Sullivan, P., Fear, J., & Joyce, P. (1997). Eating disorders and antecedent anxiety disorders: A controlled study. *Acta Psychiatrica Scandinavica, 96*, 101–107.

Bulik, C. M., Sullivan, P. F., Wade, T. D., & Kendler, K. S. (2000). Twin studies of eating disorders: A review. *International Journal of Eating Disorders, 27*, 1–20.

Bulik, C. M., Wade, T. D., & Kendler, K. S. (2001). Characteristics of monozygotic twins discordant for bulimia nervosa. *International Journal of Eating Disorders, 29*, 1–10.

Crisp, A. H. (1997). Anorexia nervosa as flight from growth: Assessment and treatment based on the model. In D. M. Garner & P. E. Garfinkel (Eds.), *Handbook of treatment for eating disorders* (pp. 248–277). New York: Guilford Press.

Crisp, A. H. (1998, May). *Anorexia nervosa: Let me be.* Presentation at Women's Mental Health Conference, New Orleans, Louisiana.

Deep, A., Nagy, L., Weltzin, T., Rao, R., & Kaye, W. (1995). Premorbid onset of psychopathology in long-term recovered anorexia nervosa. *International Journal of Eating Disorders, 17*, 291–298.

Fairburn, C. G. (1995). Binge eating and addiction. In *Overcoming binge eating* (pp. 100–111). New York: Guilford Press.

Fairburn, C. G., Cowen, P. J., & Harrison, P. J. (1999). Twin studies and the etiology of eating disorders. *International Journal of Eating Disorders, 26*, 349–358.

Feldman, W., Feldman, E., & Goodman, J. T. (1988). Culture versus biology: Children's attitudes toward thinness and fatness. *Pediatrics, 81*, 190–194.

Freeman, R. J., Thomas, C. D., Solyom, L., & Koopman, R. F. (1985). Clinical and personality correlates of body size overestimation in anorexia nervosa and bulimia nervosa. *International Journal of Eating Disorders, 4*, 439–456.

Garner, D. M., & Bemis, K. M. (1982). A cognitive-behavioral approach to anorexia nervosa. *Cognitive Therapy Research, 6*, 123–150.

Garner, D. M., Garfinkel, P. E., Schwartz, D., & Thompson, M. (1980). Cultural expectations of thinness in women. *Psychological Reports, 47*, 483–491.

Godart, N. T., Flament, M. F., Lecrubier, Y., & Jeammet, P. (2000). Anxiety disorders in anorexia nervosa and bulimia nervosa: Comorbidity and chronology of appearance. *European Psychiatry, 15*, 38–45.

Herman, C. P., & Mack, D. (1975). Restrained and unrestrained eating. *Journal of Personality, 43*, 647–660.

Hsu, L. K. G. (1990). *Eating disorders.* New York: Guilford Press.

Hudson, J. I., Laffer, D. S., & Pope, H. G., Jr. (1982). Bulimia related to affective disorder by family and response to dexamethasone suppression test. *American Journal of Psychiatry, 137*, 695–698.

Hudson, J. I., Pope, H. G., Jonas, J. M., & Yurgelun-Todd, D. (1983). Family history study of anorexia nervosa and bulimia. *British Journal of Psychiatry, 142*, 133–138.

Huon, G. F. (1994). Dieting, binge-eating, and some of their correlates among secondary school girls. *International Journal of Eating Disorders, 15*, 159–164.

Johnson, C., Steinberg, S., & Lewis, C. (1988). In K. Clark, R. Parr, & W. Castelli (Eds.), *Evaluation and management of eating disorders: Anorexia nervosa, bulimia, and obesity* (pp. 173–186). Champaign, Illinois: Life Enhancement.

Johnson-Sabine, E. C., Wood, K. H., & Wakeling, A. (1984). Mood changes in bulimia nervosa. *British Journal of Psychiatry, 145*, 512–516.

Kaye, W. H., Klump, K. L., Frank, G. K., & Strober, M. (2000). Anorexia and bulimia nervosa. *Annual Review of Medicine, 51*, 299–313.

Kaye, W., Strober, M., Stein, D., & Gendall, K. (1999). New directions in treatment research of anorexia and bulimia nervosa. *Biological Psychiatry, 45*, 1285–1292.

Klump, K. L., Kaye, W. H., & Strober, M. (2001). The evolving genetic foundations of eating disorders. *Psychiatric Clinics of North America, 24*, 215–225.

Marx, R. D. (1994). Anorexia nervosa: Theories of etiology. In L. Alexander-Mott & D. B. Lumsden (Eds.), *Understanding eating disorders: Anorexia nervosa, bulimia nervosa, and obesity* (pp. 101–117). Washington, D.C.: Taylor & Francis.

Meadow, R., & Weiss, L. (1992). *Women's conflicts about eating and sexuality: The relationship between food and sex.* Binghamton, New York: Haworth Press.

Minuchin, S., Rosman, B. L., & Baker, L. (1978). *Psychosomatic families: Anorexia nervosa in context.* Cambridge, Massachusetts: Harvard University Press.

Nasser, M. (1988). Culture and weight consciousness. *Journal of Psychosomatic Research, 32,* 573–577.

Nasser, M. (1998). Eating disorders: Between cultural specificity and globalization. *Eating Disorders Review, 9,* 1–3.

Palmer, J. (1996, July). Hey, fatso! *Barron's,* 25–29.

Pies, R. (Ed.). (1995). New directions in the diagnosis and treatment of eating disorders. *Advances in psychiatric medicine (Suppl. to Psychiatric Times).*

Pliner, P., & Haddock, G. (1996). Perfectionism in weight-concerned and unconcerned women: An experimental approach. *International Journal of Eating Disorders, 19,* 381–389.

Polivy, J. (1996). Psychological consequences of food restriction. *Journal of the American Dietetic Association, 96,* 589–592.

Powers, P. S., Schulman, R. G., Gleghorn, A. A., & Prange, M. E. (1987). Perceptual and cognitive abnormalities in bulimia. *American Journal of Psychiatry, 144,* 1456–1460.

Root, M. P., Fallon, P., & Friedrich, W. N. (1986). *Bulimia: A systems approach to treatment.* New York: W. W. Norton.

Rost, W., Neuhaus, M., & Florin I. (1982). Bulimia nervosa: Sex role attitude, sex role behavior, and sex role related locus of control in bulimarexic women. *Journal of Psychosomatic Medicine, 26,* 403–408.

Ruff, G. A., & Barrios, B. A. (1986). Realistic assessment of body image. *Behavioral Assessment, 8,* 237–251.

Selvini-Palazzoli, M. (1974). *Self starvation.* New York: Jason Aronson.

Shapiro, S., Newcomb, M., & Loeb, T. B. (1997). Fear of fat, disregulated-restrained eating, and body esteem: Prevalence and gender differences among eight- to ten-year-old children. *Journal of Clinical Child Psychology, 26,* 358–365.

Shoebridge, P., & Gowers, S. G. (2000). Parental high concern and adolescent-onset anorexia nervosa. A case-control study to investigate direction of causality. *British Journal of Psychiatry, 176,* 132–137.

Sing Lee, M. B. (1996). Clinical lessons from the cross-cultural study of anorexia nervosa. *Eating Disorders Review, 7,* 1–4.

Striegel-Moore, R. H., Silberstein, L. R., & Rodin, J. (1986). Toward an understanding of risk factors in bulimia. *American Psychologist, 41,* 246–263.

Strober, M. (1991). Family-genetic studies of eating disorders. *Journal of Clinical Psychiatry, 52* (Suppl.), 9–12.

Strober, M., Freeman, R., Lampert, C., Diamond, J., & Kaye, W. (2000). Controlled family study of anorexia nervosa and bulimia nervosa: Evidence of shared liability and transmission of partial syndromes. *American Journal of Psychiatry, 157,* 393–401.

Strober, M., Lampert, C., Morrell, W., Burroughs, J., & Jacobs, C. (1990). A controlled family study of anorexia nervosa: Evidence of familial aggregation and lack of shared transmission with affective disorders. *International Journal of Eating Disorders, 9,* 139–155.

Thompson, D. A., Berg, K. M., & Shatford, L. A. (1987). The heterogeneity of bulimic symptomology: Cognitive and behavioral dimensions. *International Journal of Eating Disorders, 6,* 215–234.

Vanderheyden, D. A., Fekken, G. C., & Boland, F. J. (1988). Critical variables associated with bingeing and bulimia in a university population: A factor analytic study. *International Journal of Eating Disorders, 7,* 321–329.

Weiss, L., Katzman, M., & Wolchik, S. (1994). Bulimia nervosa: Definition, diagnostic criteria, and associated psychological problems. In L. Alexander-Mott & D. B. Lumsden (Eds.), *Understanding eating disorders: Anorexia nervosa, bulimia nervosa, and obesity* (pp. 161–180). Washington, D.C.: Taylor & Francis.

Whitehouse, A. M., Freeman, C. L., & Annandale, A. (1986). Body size estimation in bulimia. *British Journal of Psychiatry, 149,* 98–103.

Willard, S. G. (1990). *Anorexia and bulimia: The potential devastation of dieting.* Plainfield, New Jersey: Patient Education Press.

Willard, S. G., McDermott, B. E., & Woodhouse, L. M., (1995). Lipoplasty in the bulimic patient. *Journal of Plastic and Reconstructive Surgery, 98,* 1–3.

Willmuth, M. E., Leitenberg, H., Rosen, J., Fondacaro, K. M. & Gross, J. (1985). Body size distortion in bulimia nervosa. *International Journal of Eating Disorders, 4,* 71–78.

Wilson, G. T. (1995). Eating disorders and addictive disorders. In K. D.

Brownell & C. G. Fairburn (Eds.), *Eating disorders and obesity: A comprehensive handbook* (pp. 165–170). New York: Guilford Press.

Wiseman, C. V., Gray, J. J., Mosimann, J. E., & Ahrens, A. H. (1992). Cultural expectations of thinness in women: An update. *International Journal of Eating Disorders, 11,* 85–89.

Wolf, E. M., & Crowther, J. H. (1983). Personality and eating habit variables as predictors of severity of binge eating and weight. *Addictive Behaviors, 8,* 335–344.

Woodside, D. B. (1993). Genetic contributions to eating disorders. In A. S. Kaplan & P. E. Garfinkel (Eds.), *Medical issues and the eating disorders: The interface* (pp. 193–212). New York: Brunner/Mazel.

Zerbe, K. J. (1995). *The body betrayed: A deeper understanding of women, eating disorders and treatment.* Washington, D.C.: American Psychiatric Press.

five

How Is an Eating Disorder Treated?

The anorexic patient rarely chooses to go for evaluation or treatment. It is usually the parents, spouse, or friends who insist on seeking help. The afflicted individual is typically gratified by her symptoms and they become intrinsically reinforcing. She does not therefore understand why her family and friends are so concerned. She generally feels quite successful, in fact, in her quest to be thin above all else. She often denies any problems and rejects intervention; her resistance makes treatment difficult initially. For those close to the sufferer of anorexia, the disease presents itself as a bottomless pit from which there is no obvious escape. It seems inconceivable that a person who has so much to offer chooses to destroy herself willfully in the face of family and friends, who typically wish to understand and to help. The solution seems so simple—"Just eat"—yet the problem requires a far more complex solution. The anorexic feels empty inside; her focus on food, weight, and body shape substitutes for any real feeling of self. This lack of personal identity produces frustration and fear that is undefined before treatment.

The bulimic patient, unlike the anorexic, frequently is relieved to have been discovered and to have finally admitted her problem. She tends to be motivated in psychotherapy, anxious to alleviate her symptoms and regain control of her eating. Many patients see their problem as an unfortunate habit that they cannot break and are surprised that psychotherapy is the recommended solution. It often takes weeks or months of therapy for the bulimic to realize that underlying conflicts and family issues are the true core of her illness. Most people with bulimia have repeatedly said to themselves at the beginning or conclusion of a miserable binge-purge episode, "I will never do this again." The purging feels as if a clean slate has been granted and all the damage undone, but the cycle repeats itself again and again, usually getting worse as the weeks, months, and years go by.

Eating disorders are obviously heartbreaking to everyone involved. Treatment is complicated, yet can be quite effective. The keys to successful treatment include early detection, treatment with a team of professionals who specialize in eating disorders, and compliance with recommendations of the treatment team. For assistance in locating eating disorder specialists in your area, contact the Academy for Eating Disorders, the National Eating Disorders Association, and/or the Eating Disorder Referral and Information Center, all of which are listed in Appendix A.

A MULTIDISCIPLINARY TEAM APPROACH

The treatment of eating disorders has become an important field of specialization for mental health professionals. Many major medical centers have established eating disorder clinics as the number of women requiring specialty care has escalated. As explained earlier, eating disorders are complicated illnesses that involve many different components, including psychological, social, biological, and familial. Recognition of their complexity, combined with the realization that no single discipline of health care professionals could provide comprehensive care for these patients, led to the evolution of a multidisciplinary team approach. To address all the aforementioned components, a team of experts with specific training and depth of experience in the treatment of eating disorders is necessary. A comprehensive team should include an individual psychotherapist, a nutritionist, a family therapist, a psychiatrist, and medical professionals (for example, internist, family practitioner, adolescent medicine specialist, pediatrician, gynecologist, and dentist).

Evaluation A thorough assessment is crucial to the development of an appropriate, individualized treatment plan. It is advisable to seek an evaluation from a team of experienced professionals who specialize in the treatment of eating disorders. If treatment is recommended, the professional team can determine what combination of therapies would be appropriate and most beneficial. In the case of anorexia, severity of the disease is judged on the basis of (1) degree of weight loss, (2) rate at which weight has been lost, (3) physical condition, (4) excessive caloric restriction, (5) severity of use of dietary aids such as diet pills, (6) amount of exercise, (7) psychological status, and (8) degree to which normal life has been disrupted.

Severity of bulimia is determined on the basis of (1) frequency of binge eating episodes, (2) frequency of purging behavior, (3) type of purging, such as self-induced vomiting, laxative abuse, use of enemas, emetics (syrup of ipecac), or diuretics, (4) amount of emetic, or number of laxatives or diuretics taken per purge, (5) excessive caloric restriction, (6) severity of use of dietary aids such as diet pills, (7) amount of exercise, (8) physical condition, (9) psychological status, and (10) degree to which normal life has been disrupted.

In the case of either anorexia or bulimia, if alcohol and/or other drug abuse is identified as a problem, treatment for the substance abuse will be recommended. If substance abuse is a primary problem, it should be treated first; successful treatment of an eating disorder in the presence of active substance abuse is highly unlikely, if not impossible. At times, however, it is necessary to treat the eating disorder and substance abuse simultaneously owing to the severity of the eating disorder. This concurrent treatment is best delivered in an inpatient facility that has both eating disorder and chemical dependency programs.

A thorough physical examination with laboratory workup is recommended at the outset of treatment to ascertain that no other medical problems are responsible for the eating disorder symptoms, to evaluate overall physical health, and to identify any areas of medical concern. Medical follow-up will be recommended as needed, depending on the nature and severity of the eating disorder and the patient's physical condition.

Individual Psychotherapy Individual psychotherapy is the cornerstone of the eating disorders treatment regimen. It is the therapeutic alliance between the psychotherapist and the eating disordered person that will facilitate the patient's psychological development through the "adolescent period" of emotional growth. This period may or may not coincide with the patient's actual chronological age. If it does not, the patient is nonetheless likely to experience the range and intensity of emotions typical of adolescence while progressing through treatment. At whatever age, this development will enable the affected individual to establish an identity separate from that of the family of origin, a task that typically has not been completed in the past.

To meet this goal, the psychotherapist must be unconditionally empathic, patient, and creative with treatment strategies, meaning that he or she is flexible in deeming which approach or technique is appropriate for any given therapeutic situation. We know that anorexics and bulimics are usually "empty" on the inside, having often played covertly assigned roles all their lives for the benefit of themselves and their families. The therapist must be prepared to help patients fill the gaps and remove the rigid roles as well as support the formation of independent identities. To be successful in the process, the therapist requires perseverance, in-depth understanding of the illnesses, and experience.

As explained in Chapter 4, an eating disorder provides solutions to one's problems in life and is not simply about food and weight. It may be a way of bringing parents together in a tense marriage, it may provide a legitimate reason for the affected individual to stay home instead of going off to camp or college, or it may be a means of escaping the pressures of adolescence and impending sexuality. It may also provide a feeling of accomplishment and notoriety through losing weight or be a means of "expelling" feelings through the purging process. It becomes the goal of individual psychotherapy, then, to explore the benefits and advantages of the eating disorder so that healthier ways of meeting needs can be identified, developed, learned, and maintained.

One particular means of treating the eating disordered person has to do with enabling her to get in touch with her feelings. The anorexic or bulimic typically talks in terms of "feeling fat" if it has been a "bad day," or in terms of "feeling thin" if it has been a "good day." She is shocked to learn that fat is not a feeling. Feelings are emotional states like happy, sad, or angry. Anorexics and bulimics deny themselves access to their emotional states by focusing on food, weight, and body shape. When an individual is unable to figure out what she feels, why she feels as she does, or how to have her emotional needs met in a healthy manner, it is difficult for her to form a sense of self and a cohesive identity. Hence, individual psychotherapy includes education on how to experience, identify, and express feelings. The focus of psychotherapy becomes what one psychotherapist describes as "translating the language of food and fat into the language of feelings."

This process ultimately leads to an individual's development of the personal feelings, opinions, values, beliefs, and desires that constitute who she is as a person. Another way to define this process is the development of one's identity.

In addition, individuation, interpersonal relationships, self-expression, and sexuality are common areas in need of exploration through psychotherapy. As treatment progresses and the eating disorder symptoms are relinquished, a flood of emotions and issues surfaces. The eating disordered person must learn how to cope with these emotions and issues in a healthier manner. Once the process is complete, the need to hold on to the previous symptoms disappears.

For the treatment of bulimia (or of bulimic symptoms in an anorexic), individual therapy is consistent with that described above, with the addition of more cognitive behavioral techniques that are systematically applied to eliminate behaviors such as binge eating, self-induced vomiting, and/or laxative abuse. Research has shown these techniques to be especially helpful in breaking the binge-purge cycle in the short term and at one-year follow-up. Cognitive behavioral therapy, in general, is designed to identify thought patterns and beliefs that contribute to an individual's negative feelings and maladaptive behaviors.

Erroneous reasoning patterns are common in women with eating disorders. Examples include dichotomous thinking, superstitious thinking, and personalization. Dichotomous thinking is thinking in extremes or polarities in an "all-or-none" fashion. An example is the classification of foods as either "good" or "bad," with no in-between. Superstitious thinking is having thoughts about cause-and-effect relationships that are not based on facts or evidence. A young woman with this type of thought pattern may believe that continually worrying about gaining weight will keep her from becoming heavier. Personalization is the relating of events and situations specifically to oneself. The eating disordered woman may believe, for example, that if two people are whispering, they must be talking about how fat she is. There is also a tendency to magnify, or maximize, negative events and minimize positive events that reflect on one personally. In addition to errors in reasoning, irrational beliefs are often held by eating disordered persons: "Everyone must like me" and "I must be perfect." These erroneous ways of thinking and irrational beliefs typically produce a variety of negative emotions.

When using cognitive behavioral interventions, therapist and patient identify maladaptive thoughts and beliefs, challenge them with more rational counterarguments, and replace them with adaptive thoughts and beliefs. This process is often referred to as cognitive restructuring. Other behavioral techniques used in the treatment of eating disorders include self-monitoring, behavioral contracts, and behavior management programs. Self-monitoring requires the patient to write down everything she eats, as well as other information such as time of day, events surrounding her eating, her feelings, and any other information the therapist or nutritionist deems appropriate and useful. Behavioral contracts are agreements that the patient makes with her therapist to perform or refrain from certain behaviors. In order to be effective, they should include rewards if the contract is met and negative consequences if the contract is broken. A bulimic, for example, learns how to minimize cues to binge eat, to avoid triggers to binge eating, and to substitute positive behaviors when she is aware that she is likely to binge and purge.

Behavior management programs are most frequently used in inpatient treatment settings, where the staff is trained to implement them. They may be utilized in two ways. First, the programs may be used as general inpatient protocols designed to decrease eating disordered behaviors and increase healthy coping skills. Second, they may be used to decrease or eliminate particularly problematic behavior that an individual displays and teach appropriate alternatives. The behavior may or may not be eating disorder related. For example, an adolescent girl may become verbally abusive when angry and destroy the property of others. A behavior management program could be developed to teach her anger management techniques, reward the use of such techniques, and take steps to ensure her safety and the safety of others, when necessary.

A specialized, cognitive behavioral technique for the treatment of binge eating allows the patient to eat *some* amount of a binge food, but not all. When used to treat purging behavior, the technique allows the patient to eat what she wishes, but she is not permitted to purge afterward. The resultant anxiety decreases over time, helping the patient learn that she can find ways of dealing with negative feelings other than through her self-destructive eating behaviors. A technique that uses the same principle of anxiety reduction requires the patient to wait increasingly longer periods before acting on her urges to binge and/or purge. Using the multidisciplinary approach, the nutritionist is the appropriate team member to implement these techniques, since she is the person most directly involved with food issues. The individual therapist, though, is likely to be the team member who initiates the agreement or contracts with the patient to try these techniques.

As mentioned in the previous chapter, a colleague of ours created a modified version of the twelve-step model of treatment as an adjunct to traditional, insight-oriented psychotherapy. The approach has been found to be effective with adult patients who need the structure and extensive support that the frequently offered groups provide. Teachings of the original twelve-step model that were noted to be problematic for the eating disorders population (such as abstinence from any particular food type) are not part of the program.

A specialized form of cognitive-behavioral therapy that is used to treat individuals with a variety of self-destructive behaviors is dialectical behavior therapy. This approach has been found to be quite effective in eating disorders treatment to help patients reduce or eliminate self-harm behaviors, restructure their thinking in a positive way, and generate healthy alternatives in problem-solving.

Another type of psychotherapy is eye movement desensitization reprocessing. Treatment involves suggestion and techniques similar to hypnosis. It is believed to work by reducing the anxiety provoked by disturbing events from one's life. This method appears to be widely used but does not yet have scientific support.

Interpersonal psychotherapy for bulimia is a short-term psychotherapy in which there is no discussion of the eating disorder symptoms after the assessment. Instead, treatment focuses on current interpersonal problems that maintain those symptoms. For example, it may be discovered that an argument with a friend triggers a binge eating episode followed by purging. It is the goal of this form of psychotherapy for the patient to learn how to cope with such interpersonal difficulties in a healthy fashion. Support for interpersonal psychotherapy in the treatment of bulimia has been mixed: one study showed that it was equally as effective as cognitive-behavioral therapy in reducing symptoms, while a more recent study with a larger number of patients found it to be less effective. In the treatment of anorexia, researchers have just begun to investigate the potential of interpersonal psychotherapy.

Nutritional Counseling By having a nutritionist (registered dietitian) work with the patient on food and body issues, the indivi-

COMMON ISSUES FOR INDIVIDUAL
PSYCHOTHERAPY

- Identity formation
- Individuation
- Problems of maturation and growing up
- Identification and expression of feelings
- Acceptance of feelings
- Conflict tolerance
- Sexuality
- Communication skills
- Self-esteem
- Assertiveness
- Identification and correction of negative thought patterns
- Coping skills
- Body image

dual psychotherapist is free to work with the patient to discover and resolve the underlying psychological problems. Because an eating disordered patient is obsessed with food, calories, fat grams, and her body, she needs a forum in which to air her concerns, fears, and misguided wishes. A registered dietitian who is specially trained in this area can provide the nutritional support, education, and guidance that is desperately needed. Without nutritional counseling, the patient would undoubtedly attempt to use her psychotherapy sessions to focus on food and weight. This misuse of therapy would allow her to avoid the underlying issues, just as she does in her life outside of therapy.

In nutritional counseling, a well-balanced diet is developed to achieve and maintain desired weight within certain guidelines agreed on by the patient and the dietitian. Through weekly sessions (or more often, when necessary) the patient comes to learn that her nutritionist is a reliable resource for nutrition and diet information. This contact provides support for the patient and active involvement with the nutritionist, both critical components of therapy. A long-range goal is education in sound dietary practices, with the specific objective being the establishment of new eating habits. In anorexia, of course, weight gain is the primary aim.

We have generated the following list of common topics for discussion in nutritional counseling, although the specific needs of a particular patient will vary and require tailoring the content from session to session.

Nutritional and Physiological
Sufficient caloric intake and how it is determined
Daily food plans and what they should contain
Normalization of fluid intake
Definition of a healthy weight range
Definition of a healthy body fat range
How to reach a healthy weight range
How to maintain a healthy weight range
Identification of hunger cues
Dispelling nutrition myths (for instance, that "no-fat" diets are
    healthy)
Education about metabolic rate and effects of eating disordered
    behavior (starvation, bingeing, purging)
Caloric needs when exercising
Physical dangers of herbal supplements and diet pills for
    weight control
Physical dangers of laxatives, diuretics, and syrup of ipecac for
    weight control

Normal body development
Menstruation

Behavioral
Reduction and cessation of food restriction, purging, dieting,
    and excessive exercise, as applicable
Compliance with nutritional recommendations
Normalization of eating patterns (eat when hungry, stop eating
    when full)
Normalization of eating experiences (restaurant eating, parties,
    no "special" foods)

Emotional
Learning to trust hunger cues
Identification of emotional eating or emotional restriction
Identification of triggers to emotional eating or emotional
    restriction
Body image and how it affects eating patterns

In order for nutritional counseling to be successful, development of patient-counselor rapport is crucial. In addition, it is
essential that the patient actively participate in planning her
meals. Such planning begins after an initial nutritional evaluation, which includes height, current weight, historic weight loss
or gain over time, body fat and muscle analysis, menstrual history, and percentage of weight deviation from the norm. Meal
plans are based on the American Dietetic Association's exchange
list. Calories and/or fat grams are downplayed as much as possible in favor of emphasis on exchanges. Within certain agreed-
upon guidelines, patients have substantial input into meal planning, with their personal food preferences taken into account.
Follow-up counseling sessions and observation are key if long-
term compliance is to be expected. In fact, follow-up nutritional

sessions should ideally continue until the patient no longer has any signs or symptoms of an eating disorder.

Family Therapy As previously explained, the family system is the context from which an eating disorder develops; it therefore requires change if the patient is to become free to overcome her eating disorder in that environment. For patients who are in a relatively older age range and no longer live with their families of origin, family therapy may not be required. In some cases, patients do well in treatment without any participation by their families. When a patient still lives with her family, however, family therapy is usually necessary for recovery. It is also indicated if the family lives separately but obviously functions as a stimulating factor in the illness. If the patient is married, marital therapy is often proposed as an adjunctive treatment.

Family therapy is typically geared toward understanding the role that the eating disordered daughter has characteristically played within the family system, and learning how she has contributed to whatever homeostasis has been achieved. Homeostasis refers to the balance that occurs when all family members adhere to their given, often unspoken, rules of behavior. These rules can be quite rigid, thereby preventing family members from learning more adaptive, flexible coping mechanisms in response to life stressors. As the child gets better, family therapy sometimes evolves into marital therapy for the parents, or individual therapy for one or both parents. It is not unusual for one or both of the parents to be referred for individual therapy at the outset of treatment. It sometimes is obvious that a parent's individual issues need to be addressed separately.

Group Therapy As an adjunctive form of treatment, group therapy is effective in treating bulimia. The group provides another arena in which the patient can improve her self-esteem and be-

COMMON ISSUES IN FAMILY THERAPY

- Communication problems such as lack of communication, miscommunication, direct or indirect failure to allow open expression of feelings (for instance, the message that it is not okay to be angry or upset), mixed or double messages
- Lack of appropriate parent-child boundaries (such as failure to respect privacy), enmeshment (emotional overinvolvement), disengagement (emotional distance)
- Fears around patient's growing up and becoming independent
- Roles that family members play which contribute to the development and maintenance of the eating disorder (for example, the child may be the mediator between parents in an unstable marriage)
- Control and power within the family
- Unrealistic family expectations of individual members, and of the family as a unit

come an active participant in pursuing a positive future for herself. The group can be a place where the bulimic discovers that she is not alone in the vicious cycle of bingeing and purging. The group can also give her a forum to voice her feelings, learn new coping skills, and practice relationship skills. It is often within the context of a group that a patient speaks of her illness to others for the first time, a necessary step for recovery. The bulimic typically needs, though, some amount of individual psychotherapy either prior to, or in conjunction with, group therapy.

For anorexia, outpatient group therapy can be problematic, in that the participants may become quite competitive in their pursuit of thinness, thereby stimulating and reinforcing the urge to lose weight. As a follow-up to inpatient treatment where normal weight has been attained, however, group therapy can be quite beneficial in the treatment of anorexia.

Self-help and support groups are recommended for those individuals who either are in continued treatment or have achieved recovery. But these groups *cannot* take the place of evaluation and treatment by eating disorder specialists. In the case of the individual who is still in treatment, it is important that patient and therapist agree that such groups would be beneficial to the patient's recovery efforts. In either situation, the patient is encouraged to research the type of group she is considering and to ask eating disorder professionals for recommendations. These groups vary considerably in terms of philosophy, helpfulness, leader credentials, and accuracy of information presented.

Pharmacotherapy The use of medication in the treatment of anorexia has not been found to be efficacious. Antidepressants are indicated, however, when an actual mood disorder such as depression has been diagnosed in addition to the anorexia, or when depression lingers after complete weight restoration. Certain antidepressants may help to prevent relapse in both anorexics who have reached a normal weight and in bulimics. For the treatment of bulimia, some antidepressants have been shown to be effective in decreasing binge eating and purging in the short term and in lessening depressive symptoms overall. It is essential, though, that medication not be chosen as the sole form of treatment, as medication works best in conjunction with psychotherapy. It may also be indicated for other psychiatric problems seen in conjunction with eating disorders, such as anxiety or obsessive-compulsive behaviors. The psychiatrist on the treatment team can make recommendations for psychopharmacologic treatment and follow the patient's use of medications.

Medical Consultation Because of the potentially lethal medical complications associated with both anorexia and bulimia, it is of paramount importance that the multidisciplinary team include medical personnel who recognize and understand the physical and laboratory findings associated with these disorders. In addition to physical examination and nutritional evaluation, laboratory tests can help assess the overall medical and nutritional status of the patient. Initial laboratory screenings are often recommended, but may also be necessary throughout treatment if the patient engages in laxative or diuretic abuse, frequent self-induced vomiting, use of emetics to induce vomiting, and/or has a dramatic or sudden loss of weight. Laboratory results, along with medical consultation, may aid in evaluating whether the patient can safely remain in outpatient treatment or if her condition warrants hospitalization. Other behaviors as well, such as excessive exercise or diet pill use, could compromise her health status and indicate the need for periodic medical monitoring.

Hospitalization Although the question of whether or not to hospitalize an eating disordered patient can be difficult, there are guidelines that the therapist can follow. With anorexia, the patient who presents as severely malnourished and/or emaciated (weight 20 percent or more below normal for height and body frame) should be hospitalized at the beginning of treatment, if possible. If the patient has reached 15 percent below normal weight with no medical complications, an intensive outpatient treatment regimen may be attempted initially if the patient is willing and psychologically able. Other factors, such as treatment resistance, may make a trial of intensive outpatient treatment inadvisable. A patient who has remained or stabilized at a low weight (approximately 15 percent below normal) for six months or more, and is unable or unwilling to gain weight on an outpatient basis, should be considered for inpatient treatment. A patient who began dieting at or near a normal weight and is beginning to lose at the rate of several pounds a week should also be considered for hospitalization to prevent her from reaching a state of malnutrition. Medical complications such as chemical disturbances (electrolyte imbalances), irregular or slowed heartbeats, and secondary gastrointestinal problems may also constitute criteria for hospital admission. It is prudent for patients who are admitted to a medical hospital to be transferred directly to an inpatient eating disorder unit once the medical condition is stable. Any psychological problems that might cause the individual to be a danger to herself or to others, or that greatly diminish her ability to function on a daily basis, indicate the need for inpatient treatment.

Hospitalization is recommended for bulimia when the condition is so severe that the person's day-to-day life is profoundly disturbed or the medical complications warrant inpatient treatment. Sometimes the symptoms get out of control and all the person's time is spent binge eating and purging, to the exclusion of most of life's normal activities. In this situation, hospitalization is the only way control can be regained. In addition, if a bulimic patient has severe, persistent symptoms that have not responded to an adequate trial of outpatient treatment, inpatient care is recommended.

Hospitalization is also indicated if the patient has unsuccessfully attempted to discontinue abusing laxatives or diuretics as an outpatient. When a bulimic has severely abused laxatives and/or diuretics over a long period, stopping the dosage often results in edema (swelling or bloating). Many people cannot tolerate this swelling, which they interpret as fat even though it is actually retained fluid, so they continue to repeat the laxative/diuretic cycle. These individuals often require hospitalization to stop the cycle; getting past the period of swelling and anxiety without taking laxatives or diuretics is something many bulimics cannot accomplish on their own, try as they may. Inability to stop the use of enemas and/or syrup of ipecac might also warrant hospitalization. As with anorexia, any significant psychological problems of the sort described earlier would warrant hospitalization as well.

The medical and psychiatric criteria for hospitalization should be followed by all members of the treatment team, including the patient and her family. This type of unity prevents misunderstandings and ensures a smooth transition to inpatient treatment. To facilitate the process, frequent communication regarding the possibility of hospitalization must take place among all parties involved. The psychotherapist is the person who explains the criteria to the patient, but it is often either the nutritionist or the treating physician who actually informs the patient when inpatient treatment is imperative. The nutritionist is most often the person who informs the patient when psychiatric hospitalization on an eating disorder unit is recommended, because she is the team member who regularly monitors the patient's weight and eating behaviors. If possible, the nutritionist and the psychotherapist should inform the patient together that she has failed to meet the criteria set by the treatment team for outpatient treatment. When laboratory values, an electrocardiogram, or other medical evidence provide sufficient cause for medical hospitalization, the treating physician is the team member likely to inform the patient that she needs to be admitted medically.

Therapeutically, having the admission orchestrated by the nutritionist or the physician works in favor of the individual psychotherapist, because it lessens the probability of damage to the therapeutic alliance. Patients often become angry when told they must be hospitalized, despite the fact that they have been aware of the criteria from the start. Their anger is usually directed toward the person who informs them of the necessity for hospitalization. Minor setbacks in therapeutic alliances with the nutritionist and/or the treating physician can be tolerated better than setbacks with the psychotherapist. In most cases, these relationships are quickly healed and restored to prehospitalization status. Patients are also likely to become temporarily angry with family members and friends who support the hospitalization. Most patients, though, also feel some degree of relief when the pending question of hospitalization is ultimately resolved. If hospitalization is required because of a psychiatric emergency, the individual therapist would be the team member to inform the patient, as the emergency would probably be identified in the psychotherapist's office. If the emergency is identified by the psychiatrist, however, he or she would initiate hospitalization.

Up to now, we have discussed inpatient treatment in terms of full-time psychiatric hospitalization. Two other types of inpatient treatment regimens serve different, often complimentary purposes: partial hospitalization programs and residential treatment programs. Partial hospitalization is often needed as a bridge between full-time hospital care and outpatient treatment. It may also be an option for someone who needs more than outpatient care but does not meet the criteria for full-time hospitalization. Partial programs, sometimes called day hospital programs, are usually conducted from morning to evening hours, with full treatment available during that time. The patient goes home for the evening and returns the next day. These programs may or may not offer weekend care and may or may not provide all meals and snacks. Residential programs, on the other hand, are intended for individuals who need long-term care. There are various levels of supervision, allowing the patient long-term, comprehensive treatment they require to return to a healthy, productive life. If you or someone you know is unable to see an eating disorders specialist because of this type of problem, encourage the holder of the insurance plan to contact his or her employer (or whoever pays the premiums) to lobby for approval of the needed treatment. It may be possible to transfer dollar amounts of "medical benefits" over to "psychiatric benefits" to obtain the needed coverage. Many patients and their families have been quite successful with an aggressive approach of this sort. It may also be helpful to contact the state insurance commissioner or to enlist the support of eating disorder advocacy groups (see the list in Appendix A).

A colleague has compiled a list of ten specific arguments, all backed by scientific research, that may be presented to insurance companies in support of coverage for eating disorder treatment. The list is available on the National Eating Disorders Association website (again, see Appendix A). In addition, she has compiled steps to follow in navigating the private and governmental systems in order to obtain needed care; these steps are listed on the same website.

If these strategies fail, it may be worthwhile to check with the nearest universities or university medical centers that have an eating disorders clinic. Often, they have students in training who will see patients for greatly reduced fees. Some universities also provide free treatment in conjunction with their research programs. Certain criteria must generally be met in order to participate in these programs, and space may be limited. Contact the Academy for Eating Disorders or Anorexia Nervosa and Related Eating Disorders for information on research-based treatment programs (see Appendix A). We are aware of a few individuals who contacted state government officials, presented their plight, and were subsequently granted state-funded treatment. The state of Minnesota set an important legal precedent in June

to reduce the amount of structure gradually as she becomes more proficient at taking care of herself. These programs are usually set in a rather home-like environment so that the patient can learn to transition to her own home.

Below we give criteria for the appropriate level of care. These are meant to serve as *general* guidelines only. Each individual's case is unique and may require a different level of care based on current psychological and medical condition, family situation, support system, and history of illness.

Inpatient
Severe malnourishment (weight 20 percent or more below
    normal for height and body frame)
Medical complications
Psychiatric emergency (such as thoughts of suicide)
Inability to perform routine functions (for example, unable to
    go to school or work, unable to care for self)
Persistent, severe symptoms that do not respond to outpatient
    treatment
Inability to stop use of laxatives, diuretics, enemas, or syrup of
    ipecac
Rapid decline in weight
Rapid worsening of symptoms indicating loss of control

Outpatient
Cooperative with treatment plan and recommendations
Ability to take care of self on daily basis
Capable of achieving and maintaining a healthy weight
Psychiatrically stable
Medically stable

Partial Hospitalization (Day Hospital) Program
Failure to respond to outpatient treatment but failure to meet
    criteria for inpatient treatment

Need for transition from inpatient care to outpatient treatment
Inability to perform routine daily functions
Ability to care for self during evening hours and overnight
Cooperative with treatment plan and treatment
    recommendations
Psychiatrically stable
Medically stable

Residential Treatment Program
High risk of relapse in partial program or outpatient treatment
Long-term, continued treatment required
Inability to perform routine daily functions
Psychiatrically unstable
Medically stable

ASSESSMENT OF TREATMENT QUALITY

Trying to obtain eating disorder treatment for yourself or a loved one is an emotionally charged goal, and it can be very difficult to determine objectively the quality of care provided by various programs. This is especially true if conflicting recommendations are made by different health care professionals. In an attempt to assist people in assessing quality of care, we have compiled a list of questions to ask and things to look for in obtaining sound treatment.

Questions to Ask
What are your credentials?
What specialized training do you have in treatment of eating
    disorders?
To which professional eating disorder association do you
    belong?
What approach do you use to treat eating disorders, and do you
    work as part of a team with other professionals?

How often do you communicate with the other professionals
    involved in treatment?

What to Look for in Quality Care
Appropriate credentials. Contact the organizations listed in
    Appendix A for referrals.
Multidisciplinary treatment. In rural areas, this may mean the
    involvement of professionals who are not necessarily in close
    physical proximity. Through effective communication and
    treatment planning, it is still possible for the professionals to
    work as a team.
Attention to the psychological reasons for the eating disorder
    and to stopping the behavioral symptoms (starvation, refusal
    to maintain a normal weight, purging, and the like).

Successful treatment requires that all aspects of the eating disorder be treated. An exception is interpersonal psychotherapy for bulimia. It does not address the eating problem directly, yet has been shown to be helpful in reducing symptoms. If the individual does not improve with this form of therapy, we strongly recommend using an approach that directly addresses the eating problem as well as the psychosocial issues. By definition of these illnesses, the affected person is not truly well until the behavioral symptoms are gone.

INSURANCE COVERAGE

Managed care has greatly impacted mental health services. Many plans refuse to cover specialty care such as treatment of eating disorders. Furthermore, the insurance companies that do cover this type of care often impose limitations on providers, hospitalization benefits, and outpatient visits. These, as well as other obstacles put forth by various companies, have made it financially difficult or even impossible for many patients to procure the

2000 for the treatment of eating disorders: as the result of a lawsuit filed by that state's attorney general, Minnesota Blue Cross and Blue Shield agreed to cover inpatient treatment of eating disorders. In sum, we strongly encourage patients and families to take a proactive stance to obtain the care they need and deserve.

GETTING AND STAYING WELL

Many people who have eating disorders, and their families, deny these illnesses until the problems become extremely severe. It is extraordinarily difficult for the seemingly ideal family to admit to a serious emotional problem in their presumably perfect daughter. In a family of this type, the daughter is not expected to have difficulties; she is supposed to be the ideal child who gives the family nothing but pleasure. Thus, getting the afflicted person into treatment and keeping her there is often difficult. Once into treatment, both the patient and the family usually come to appreciate the supportive and caring environment that therapy offers. They realize early in treatment that the prospects for recovery and restored normalcy are far more promising with their full cooperation and participation. The earlier the treatment, the better the prognosis. The longer the behaviors and attitudes associated with the eating disorder persist, the more difficult it becomes to overcome the illness. Early and comprehensive intervention frequently means relatively short-term treatment and full recovery. Unfortunately, the converse is also true: delayed intervention can mean long-term treatment with disappointing results or even death.

Response to treatment for the eating disorders ranges from negligible to complete recovery. It involves not only weight gain or cessation of abnormal eating/purging behaviors, but also the return to a normal social and emotional life. No firm conclusions can be reached about recovery rates, owing to the relatively small number of studies in this area as well as problems that plague some of the existing research. The problems include: small samples, study design flaws, varying definitions of eating disorders and of recovery, differences in how outcome is rated, variations in the type of inpatient and outpatient treatment received, differences in individual patient characteristics and circumstances, and withdrawal of patients from the studies. These problems account for the wide range of recovery rates that is seen in the literature, and can mislead people in an overly positive or overly negative direction. Recent studies have attempted to correct some of these problems, but the reports cited below must be read with caution and are not definitive indicators of any particular individual's chance of getting well.

A review of outcome studies with anorexics determined that, in general, a bit more than 40 percent of those with anorexia recover fully, roughly a third improve but still have symptoms, and about 20 percent remain chronically ill. Another study conducted with a severely ill group of anorexics found only a 24 percent full recovery rate after ten years. From the same study, a little more than a quarter normalized weight and menstrual cycle, but continued to have problems with body image and/or abnormal eating. Forty-five percent remained ill, and the death rate was almost 7 percent. The patients had been hospitalized for an average of thirty-five days initially, and the type of subsequent treatment varied.

Another study found that 33 percent of patients fully recovered after seven and a half years; when partial recovery was included, 83 percent improved. Approximately one third relapsed after full recovery.

A six-year outcome study with anorexics conducted in Germany showed that at follow-up 55 percent recovered, approximately 10 percent were bulimic with purging, 2 percent had an unspecified eating disorder, and close to 27 percent remained ill. The death rate was almost 6 percent. These patients received long-term, intensive inpatient treatment, but did not have much access to follow-up outpatient care because of the health care system. In addition, they did not receive treatment until an average of six years after the onset of their anorexia.

An Australian study found that 56 percent had no diagnosable eating disorder five years after inpatient treatment. Three of ninety-five patients died. Finally, an American long-term study conducted with severely ill adolescents found that after fifteen years, almost 76 percent had fully recovered, 11 percent had partially recovered, and 14 percent remained ill. Relapse following full recovery was rare and those patients who relapsed did not meet all criteria for an eating disorder, although some symptoms were present. All patients received early and intensive inpatient treatment at a university-based medical center. Weight was restored to 90–95 percent of normal weight, and the patients received outpatient treatment after hospitalization.

Recovery rates are higher for bulimics than for anorexics. One review of short- and long-term studies taken together indicated that about one half of individuals with bulimia recovered, approximately 30 percent retained some symptoms, and 20 percent remained actively bulimic. Recent long-term studies show more favorable results.

One investigation showed a full recovery rate of 74 percent after seven and a half years, and a partial recovery rate of 99 percent. About one third of the sample relapsed after full recovery. Similarly, a six-year follow-up study done in Germany found a 71 percent recovery rate. Patients received primarily intensive inpatient treatment. A little greater than 21 percent of the subjects remained bulimic after six years, close to 4 percent became anorexic, about 1 percent developed binge eating disorder, and a little over 1.5 percent had an unspecified eating disorder. Two patients of the original 196 died. Another study found that close to 70 percent of bulimics were either partially or fully recovered after approximately eleven and a half years, while about 11 percent were still bulimic. Eighteen and one-half percent had an unspecified eating disorder and a very small percentage became anorexic. Finally, an Australian investigation found that 74 percent of bulimics recovered fully after five years.

Although it is difficult to precisely determine the percentages of individuals who recover, we know that recovery is possible. We also know that it is not unusual for therapy to be very long term, lasting two to five years or more. Often patients and/or families become frustrated and leave treatment prematurely, feeling that it is useless to continue when symptoms are not resolved quickly. It feels easier for the person with the illness to give up the seemingly fruitless effort of treatment and return to the former solution of using her body to cope with problems. It is therefore crucial for families and friends to promote and support perseverance. Convincing someone with anorexia or bulimia not only to begin treatment, but to continue for as long as necessary, can save her life. Outcome studies have demonstrated how complex these illnesses are, and that many different characteristics and circumstances can affect a positive or negative outcome. Getting well may take a long time—with periods of slow progress, no progress, or even relapse. For all parties involved, it is essential during the tough times to continue the commitment to getting well and remaining healthy.

Selected Bibliography

Agras, W. S., Rossiter, E. M., Arnow, B., Schneider, J. A., Telch, C. F., Raeburn, S. D., Bruce, B., Perl, M., & Koran, L. M. (1992). Pharmacologic and cognitive-behavioral treatment for bulimia nervosa: A controlled comparison. *American Journal of Psychiatry, 149,* 82–87.
Agras, W. S., Rossiter, E. M., Arnow, B., Telch, C. F., Raeburn, S. D.,

Bruce, B., & Koran, L. M. (1994). One-year follow-up of psychosocial and pharmacologic treatments for bulimia nervosa. *Journal of
Clinical Psychiatry, 55,* 179–183.

Agras, W. S., Walsh, B. T., Fairburn, C. G., Wilson, G. T., & Kraemer, H.
C. (2000). A multicenter comparison of cognitive-behavioral therapy and interpersonal psychotherapy for bulimia nervosa. *Archives
of General Psychiatry, 57,* 459–466.

Ben-Tovim, D. I., Walker, K., Gilchrist, P., Freeman, R., Kalucy, R., &
Esterman, A. (2001). Outcome in patients with eating disorders: A
5-year study, *Lancet, 357,* 1254–1257.

Cooper, P. J., & Steere, J. (1995). A comparison of two psychological
treatments for bulimia nervosa: Implications for models of maintenance. *Behavior Research and Therapy, 33,* 875–885.

Corsini, R. B. (1984). *Counseling theories and methods* (p. 551). New York:
Bantam.

Eckert, E. D., Halmi, K. A., Marchi, P., Grove, W., & Crosby, R. (1995).
Ten-year follow-up of anorexia nervosa: Clinical course and outcome. *Psychological Medicine, 25,* 143–156.

Fairburn, C. G., & Hay, P. J. (1992). The treatment of bulimia nervosa.
Annals of Medicine, 24, 297–302.

Fairburn, C. G., Jones, R., Peveler, R. C., Carr, S. J., Solomon, R. A.,
O'Connor, M. E., Burton, J., & Hope, R. A. (1991). Three psychologi-
cal treatments for bulimia nervosa: A comparative trial. *Archives of
General Psychiatry, 48,* 463–469.

Fichter, M. M., & Quadflieg, N. (1997). Six-year course of bulimia nervosa. *International Journal of Eating Disorders, 22,* 361–384.

Garner, D. M., & Bemis, K. M. (1982). A cognitive-behavioral approach
to anorexia nervosa. *Cognitive Therapy Research, 6,* 123–150.

Goldner, E. M., & Birmingham, C. L. (1994). Anorexia nervosa: Methods of treatment. In L. Alexander-Mott & D. B. Lumsden (Eds.),
*Understanding eating disorders: Anorexia nervosa, bulimia nervosa and
obesity* (pp. 135–157). Washington, D.C.: Taylor & Francis.

Hatsukami, D. (1985). Behavioral treatment of anorexia nervosa and
bulimia. In J. E. Mitchell (Ed.), *Anorexia nervosa and bulimia: Diagnosis
and treatment* (pp. 105–133). Minneapolis: University of Minnesota
Press.

Herzog, D. B., Dorer, D. J., Keel, P. K., Selwyn, S. E., Ekeblad, E. R., Flores, A. T., Greenwood, D. N., Burwell, R. A., & Keller, M. B. (1999). Recovery and relapse in anorexia and bulimia nervosa: A 7.5-year follow-up study. *Journal of the American Academy of Adolescent Psychiatry, 38*, 829–837.

Hsu, L. K. G. (1995). Outcome of bulimia nervosa. In K. D. Brownell & C. G. Fairburn (Eds.), *Eating disorders and obesity* (pp. 238–244). New York: Guilford Press.

Hudson, J. I., Chase, E. A., & Pope, H. G. (1998). Eye movement desensitization and reprocessing in eating disorders: Caution against premature acceptance. *International Journal of Eating Disorders, 23*, 1–5.

Johnson, C. L., & Sansone, R. A. (1993). Integrating the twelve-step approach with traditional psychotherapy for the treatment of eating disorders. *International Journal of Eating Disorders, 14*, 121–134.

Keel, P. K., Mitchell, J. E., Miller, K. B., Davis, T. L., & Crow, S. J. (1999). Long-term outcome of bulimia nervosa. *Archives of General Psychiatry, 56*, 63–69.

Linehan, M. M. (1993). *Cognitive-behavioral treatment of borderline personality disorder.* New York: Guilford Press.

McIntosh, V. V., Bulik, C. M., McKenzie, J. M., Luty, S. E., & Jordan, J. (2000). Interpersonal psychotherapy for anorexia nervosa. *International Journal of Eating Disorders, 27*, 125–139.

Romano, S. J., Halmi, K. A., Sarkar, N. P., Koke, S. C., & Lee, J. S. (2002). A placebo-controlled study of fluoxetine in continued treatment of bulimia nervosa after successful acute fluoxetine treatment. *American Journal of Psychiatry, 159*, 96–102.

Stein, D., & Kaye, W. H. (1998). Using antidepressants to treat eating disorders. *Eating Disorders Review, 9*, 1–5.

Steinhausen, H. C. (1995). The course and outcome of anorexia nervosa. In K. D. Brownell & C. G. Fairburn (Eds.), *Eating disorders and obesity* (pp. 234–237). New York: Guilford Press.

Stephenson, J. N., Ohlrich, E. S., McClintock, J. H., Foster, S. W., Reinke, J. A., Allen, M. E., & Giles, G. M. (1988). The multidisciplinary team approach to the treatment of eating disorders in youth. In K. Clark, R. Parr, & W. Castelli (Eds.), *Evaluation and man-*

vicariously through their children and their children's successes and accomplishments. When these youngsters start to show signs of puberty or adolescence, the parents often get depressed or frightened about what the future will hold when the children are fully grown and gone. The unconscious pressure on these children is to stay young and not grow up. Family loyalty to maintaining the status quo is often chosen over normal development, which would lead to separation and independence.

Other characteristics that may be present in some form include a critical parent, one or more parents with depression, and/or the presence of marital problems (which may give the child the spoken or unspoken message that if she grows up and becomes independent, the family system will fall apart).

In summary, the family may contribute to the development of an eating disorder by providing an environment that can hinder a girl or young woman from establishing an identity, from practicing effective communication skills, and/or from learning adaptive coping strategies. Within the context of the family, an eating disorder may help her establish an identity separate from the family (i.e., the eating disorder becomes her identity), cope with stressors, distract her from negative feelings, and provide what she considers to be a means of safe self-expression.

THE ADDICTION MODEL

One proposed explanation of eating disorders is that they are an addiction or chemical dependency, similar to alcoholism or other drug addiction. This concept seems especially valid when one considers the binge eating seen in anorexia and bulimia— although in anorexia, sufferers are said to be "addicted" to starvation. Proponents of this model point out that in both drug addiction and eating disorders, individuals deny the problem, continue the behaviors despite adverse consequences, make re-

agement of eating disorders: Anorexia, bulimia, and obesity (pp. 261–278). Champaign, Illinois: Life Enhancement.

Strober, M., Freeman, R., & Morrell, W. (1997). The long-term course of severe anorexia nervosa in adolescents: Survival analysis of recovery, relapse, and outcome predictors over 10–15 years in a prospective study. *International Journal of Eating Disorders, 22,* 339–360.

Walsh, T. (1995). New directions in the diagnosis and treatment of eating disorders. *Advances in psychiatric medicine* (Suppl. to *Psychiatric Times*).

Weiss, L., Katzman, M., & Wolchik, S. (1999). Group therapy for bulimia nervosa. In R. Lemberg (Ed.) with L. Cohn, *Eating disorders: A reference sourcebook* (pp. 113–120). Phoenix, Arizona: Oryx Press.

Willard, S. G. (1990). *Anorexia and bulimia: The potential devastation of dieting.* Plainfield, New Jersey: Patient Education Press.

Willard, S. G., Anding, R. H., & Winstead, D. K. (1983). Nutritional counseling as an adjunct to psychotherapy in bulimia treatment. *Psychosomatics, 24,* 541–545.

Willard, S. G., & Winstead, D. K. (1984). Treating bulimia: A combined therapy approach. *Clinical Social Work Journal, 12,* 225–232.

six

What Can Family, Friends, and Others Do to Help?

As mentioned throughout this book, convincing someone with an eating disorder to admit that she has a problem and persuading her to seek help can be a daunting task. The person's life, however, can depend on someone's stepping in to take necessary action when she cannot, or will not, help herself.

INTERVENTION

For family members, it is often imperative to use whatever resources are at your disposal to escort the individual to an evaluation. Keep in mind that intervention with someone who is in the throes of an eating disorder is usually more of a process than a one-time event. Family members who notice suspicious behaviors may eventually have to take concrete steps toward getting help (schedule an evaluation, for instance) if the individual remains in denial. If you have specific questions about how to handle this type of situation, we strongly encourage you to consult eating disorder specialists in your area. If you do not know of any nearby, contact the Academy for Eating Disorders, the National Eating Disorders Association, and/or the Eating Disorder

Referral and Information Center, all of which are listed in Appendix A. The National Eating Disorders Association also has helpful tips on how to approach the individual about whom you have concerns.

Family Members If you are a parent, it is best to discuss your concerns with your daughter before the evaluation and inform her of the appointment. Set aside a time to talk when neither of you is rushed, and think ahead of time about what you want to say. Some parents write themselves notes so that they will remember all the concerns that they want to express. If your daughter does not agree with you, she may attempt to talk you out of your sentiments or she may become angry. Do not allow her reaction to alter your decision; if you suspect an eating disorder, you obviously have reasons for your concerns. Explain to your daughter that professionals can determine whether or not a problem exists, and assure her that if no problem is found, the issue will be considered resolved.

Many parents are tempted to keep the plan for an evaluation from their daughter in order to avoid a confrontation. Secrecy is not a good idea. It is only likely to increase anger and distrust, often making for a hostile evaluation environment. If your daughter is of legal age and does not want to go for an evaluation, ask yourself if there are any resources you could draw upon. Some parents have successfully appealed to their children's schools to assist them in their endeavor to seek help. If you financially support her college education, you might have to make the monetary support contingent on her getting help. Whatever means you choose to assure that an evaluation takes place, present your choice in a caring, empathic manner so that your daughter will know that your primary concern is her welfare.

If you are a sibling or an extended-family member, it is important that you alert the child's parents of your concerns. When

they intervene, you may be asked to join them in the intervention. In the extreme case, if an adult child's life is in immediate
danger and she refuses help, a parent, spouse, or other relative
may have to seek legal assistance to obtain treatment against the
person's will. This step is very difficult for all involved, yet may
be required if the individual's life hangs in the balance. Consultation with health care professionals is recommended if you are
considering this option.

Friends If you are a friend of someone you suspect has an eating disorder, express your concerns to your friend and encourage
her to seek help. If other friends also have concerns, you could
express them together so that she understands that a number of
people observe the problem. Always approach your friend in a
supportive, caring, nonthreatening manner. Do not be surprised
if she does not respond to your concerns in the way you would
like. If she denies a problem, becomes angry, and/or refuses to
seek help, consider seeking assistance. You may want to speak
to her family or contact a school counselor, teacher, or coach. If
you are a minor, it is best to confide in an adult whom you trust
to assist you with your efforts. Tackling such a serious situation
on your own is a heavy burden.

Teachers and Coaches Teachers and coaches can have a powerful
impact on students. Specifically, they spend a great deal of time
with young people, have the opportunity to see how students
interact with peers and others on a daily basis, and in some cases
may be more objective than family members. Furthermore, a
teacher or coach may be an adult with whom the adolescent
feels comfortable sharing troublesome thoughts and feelings.
For these reasons, it is not unusual for teachers and coaches to
be faced with the dilemma of what to do if they know or suspect that one of their students has an eating disorder. In order

to effectively intervene, we suggest that you enlist the assistance of the school counselor.

If you are the person who knows of, or suspects, a problem, approach the student in a caring manner and express your concerns. Inform her that you would like her to meet with you and the school counselor. Tell her what you plan to tell the counselor, so as to maintain a positive relationship. If the student resists the idea, in a supportive way insist on the meeting. Explain that if an evaluation reveals that there is not really a problem, the matter will be considered over. Brief the school counselor before the meeting takes place, so that he or she knows what to expect and you can work together to assist the student.

When the meeting takes place, express your concerns to the counselor in front of the student. It is important to have a plan of action ready to implement. The plan should include inviting the parents to come in so that they can be notified of the problem with all parties present. A plan of action is very important in order to (1) impart the seriousness of the situation and (2) ease the anxiety that accompanies it.

The plan will also necessitate an eating disorder evaluation. We recommend that the evaluation be conducted by a team of eating disorder specialists whenever possible, including a mental health professional and a nutritionist. School counselors who do not have experience dealing with students who have eating disorders should refer to Chapter 8 for detailed information on eating disorder evaluation, referral, and treatment.

The type of intervention detailed above assumes that the student is a minor. If she is a young adult of legal age, the process may need to change somewhat—especially if the student is reluctant to admit a problem and/or seek help. Some schools, for reasons of confidentiality, may choose not to notify parents immediately. The severity of the problem, however, may necessitate parental notification. There has been legal controversy about what steps a university may take to ensure that a student is medically safe while on campus. Nevertheless, we recommend that a family meeting take place with university personnel whenever possible so that plans for evaluation and treatment can be developed and implemented in a timely manner. Family involvement is crucial for a successful outcome. It is also wise to contact the nearest eating disorder specialist for advice on how to intervene in a particular case.

PARTICIPATION IN TREATMENT

Family   Peer relationships are crucial during the stage of development between childhood, when the family is the main resource for meeting children's needs, and adulthood, when nonfamilial resources are paramount. During adolescence, it is important for friends to become the primary interest and for the family to take a back seat. So often an eating disordered patient and her mother describe each other as "my best friend." This mutual dependency inhibits the development of normal peer relationships, thus depriving the young girl of appropriate "growing-up" experiences. Without a peer group, it is next to impossible for her to make the necessary transition from her family to the larger world. The eating disorder often legitimates the patient's remaining within the family as a small, underdeveloped, or sickly child. Whether this refusal to grow up is to meet the needs of the family, the child, or both, it is abnormal and potentially life threatening. Development of friendships and immersion in the peer world is essential to preventing or correcting an eating disorder.

Family therapy is a critical component of treatment, as the family is the context out of which eating disorders arise. Because these illnesses take such a devastating toll on family members, family therapy must be an integral part of the treatment plan.

It is never useful or appropriate to blame anyone for development of an eating disorder. Rather, the larger picture must be
examined in order to make sense of the family dynamics that
have precipitated and maintained the symptoms. Parents need
support and advice on how to deal with these complex disorders
that are so hard to understand. They need help sorting out the
patterns of behavior and resolving the relational conflicts that
are contributing to maintenance of the illness, so that changes
can be made which will ultimately free the patient to recover.
No two families are alike, and the multiple causes of an eating
disorder are never clear-cut, but working as a family to restore
health is always advisable. Even if the afflicted individual is older
and no longer living with her parents, family therapy (including marital or couples therapy, if applicable) is recommended
whenever possible.

When family members refuse to participate in recommended
treatment, a clear message is sent to the one suffering with the
eating disorder. The patient hears that she alone is the one with
a problem. Family refusal to participate in treatment and/or to
cooperate with treatment recommendations can have a devastating effect. If the family disagrees with some aspect of the
treatment or treatment recommendations, those involved can
meet with the family therapist, or the entire treatment team
if need be, to work out those differences. This sort of reaction
models adaptive coping skills for the family and for the person with the illness. It also creates an atmosphere of mutual
cooperation and respect in which healing can take place. If, however, the family views the treatment team adversarily, a successful outcome is jeopardized.

Friends At times a patient may wish to involve friends and significant others who are not family members in her treatment. Such
involvement can be highly beneficial for the person undergoing

treatment, and it can strengthen her relationships. Friends asked to attend such sessions may feel a bit uneasy initially, but typically find the experience to be rewarding.

SUPPORT AND UNDERSTANDING

Family Besides treatment by a team of professionals, a patient's recovery is greatly enhanced by support and understanding of her family. Parents need to recognize that attempting to force their anorexic daughter to eat or following their bulimic child to the bathroom after a meal will only aggravate the problem. For example, when parents coerce their daughter to eat, it is likely to make her all the more determined to starve herself.

The afflicted person is, through her illness, making a statement about her identity, her autonomy, and her quest for independence. For whatever reason, she has felt controlled by her environment, unable to be her own person. She has turned to her body to experience the control she feels she has lost or has never had. She must be given the freedom to pursue life on her own terms, to live for herself and not through or for others. Encouragement of independent decision-making, and recognition for formulation and expression of original thoughts and ideas, are healthy responses to her attempts at autonomous thinking. Her submissive behavior before the onset of her illness, her thoughtful gestures, and her willingness to go along with the crowd always made her easy to be around, a pleasure to know and love. But perpetuating and encouraging these behaviors only inhibits her self-discovery and prevents her from formulating her own values.

Friends Friends are tempted to talk about calories and food to the "successful" dieter. It is common for them to question their anorexic or bulimic friend and ask about her "secrets" for weight loss. This sort of talk is not helpful; to the contrary, it is anxiety provoking and highlights the anorexic's sense of superiority regarding her disease and the bulimic's sense of shame. Anorexics often describe their starvation as "the only thing I can do well" or "the only thing that makes me happy." Dwelling on the symptoms increases these feelings and encourages continuation of the problem behavior.

It is best to avoid nagging or questioning the eating disordered friend about food. Instead, focus on getting her out among friends and having fun in normal ways for her age. She may have a problem pursuing others or asking for companionship. She may isolate herself, repeatedly refusing invitations to go on outings. Most helpful is when friends insist on having her join them, refusing to take no for an answer. If she is treated as an important, worthwhile person, she will eventually believe herself to be one. She needs a forum in which to express herself, to discover her own unique personality. Relating to her friends in a normal fashion provides an appropriate context within which she can have an opportunity to evolve. A recovering patient put her illness in perspective as she said, "It's not worth going through all the pain I've been through, when what I needed to do all along was to express my real feelings to my friends and family, instead of looking to weight loss to solve my problems."

Teachers, School Counselors, and Coaches   The incorporation of a trusted teacher, school counselor, and/or coach into the team of professionals assisting an adolescent or young adult in recovery from an eating disorder can be a tremendous asset. All these professionals are in a position to observe how the young woman is functioning in the school environment and may be privy to concerns that the student would not share with unfamiliar mem-

bers of the mental health treatment team. If her illness has required hospitalization, these professionals can aid the eating
disordered individual when it is time to assimilate back into her
natural environment.

Incorporation of willing school personnel requires consent
from the legal guardians of a minor and, preferably, agreement
of the student as well. The role of the designated school official
in the student's treatment will be determined by the patient and
her treatment team. For example, if a student is returning to
school after hospitalization, she may need to know that someone is there for her to talk with if she has a rough day. She may
also need someone to inform other staff about how to interact
with her in order to allow her to focus on resuming a normal
school experience.

For this approach to be successful, communication between
school personnel and the individual psychotherapist is essential.
In our experience, students are relieved to know that someone
at school has an idea of what their struggles entail. For more
details on the multidisciplinary treatment of eating disorders,
see Chapter 5, and for information on the role of schools and
school curricula in the prevention of eating disorders, contact
the National Eating Disorders Association (Appendix A).

Individuals who develop eating disorders are often "the cream
of the crop," the brightest and most successful of young women.
It is a waste, indeed, for them to sacrifice themselves to these
cruel, relentless illnesses. Although recovery may be slow, perhaps even several years or more, a healthy body, mind, and life
can be restored. With timely, appropriate, and complete treatment—coupled with support and encouragement from family
and friends—eating disorders can be cured and happy, normal
lives resumed.

HOW TO BE HELPFUL

Things You Can Do

- Acknowledge the individual with an eating disorder as a person with interests, opinions, values, achievements, and life events that do not involve the eating disorder. This approach helps the person develop her sense of self and encourages her to let go of the eating disorder as her identity.
- If you are a family member, discuss any concerns regarding eating disordered behavior in family therapy. If you are a friend, direct your concerns to the individual first and then ask if she would like you to attend a family therapy session to express them. See the beginning of this chapter if the person you are concerned about is not in treatment.
- Allow the person with an eating disorder to be responsible for healthy eating behavior.
- Have family meals at least once a day and strive to make them pleasant for all.
- Be a healthy role model in terms of food, exercise, weight, and body shape.

Things You Should Not Do

- Do not comment on weight or focus on appearance. Such comments, regardless of the intention, are likely to have a negative effect. (For example, "You look so much better since you've gained weight" will be interpreted as "You are fat." "You look great" may be heard as "You have gained weight and are therefore fat.") Say how delighted you are to see the person, talk to the person, and so on.

HOW TO BE HELPFUL   *continued*

- Do not focus on eating disordered behavior. Do not ask what the person has or has not eaten, or if she has engaged in unhealthy behaviors (such as purging or excessive exercise). Avoid discussion of eating behaviors to help the individual be responsible for her own behavior and help her let go of the eating disorder as her identity.
- Refrain from allowing the person to cook for the entire household and/or prepare special meals, especially if they involve food she will not eat.
- Do not prepare separate meals for the individual or be a "short-order cook." It is important for the person to learn to stop creating an isolative mealtime experience by eating different, "special" food items. It is vital to diminish her identity as the family member "with the eating disorder." Acceptable shopping lists can be discussed prior to mealtimes.
- Refrain from criticizing your own appearance and that of others. Do not compliment others solely on the way they look, as this focus only encourages the individual to base her own self-worth on appearance.

Selected Bibliography

Eating Disorders Awareness and Prevention. (1998). *How to help a friend with eating and body image issues.* Seattle: Author.

Siegel, M., Brisman, J., & Weinshel, M. (1997). *Surviving an eating disorder: Perspective and strategies for families and friends* (Revised Ed.). New York: HarperCollins.

seven

Are Eating Disorders Different in Males?

The largest discrepancy between males and females in the diagnosis of psychiatric illnesses occurs among eating disorders, where males are in the vast minority. The males who are affected, however, suffer no less than females and, perhaps, in some ways more. Although many signs, symptoms, and features of eating disorders are shared, important differences result from gender. In this chapter, we will first describe the prevalence and onset of eating disorders in males, then highlight the similarities and differences between males and females with regard to development and treatment. It must be noted that relatively little research has been conducted in this area and much remains unknown. For readers interested in additional information on this topic, see A. E. Anderson, *Males with Eating Disorders*, and A. E. Anderson, L. Cohn, and T. Holbrook, *Making Weight: Healing Men's Conflicts with Food, Weight and Shape*.

PREVALENCE AND ONSET

As explained in an earlier chapter, the prevalence of diagnosable eating disorders in males is estimated to be one male for every ten females. Some researchers believe that the ratio is as high as one to six. Males may also suffer from "reverse anorexia," in which they fear thinness and strive for increased muscle mass. In cases of anorexia occurring before puberty, boys constitute approximately 20–25 percent of diagnosed cases. Thus, the gender gap at that age is not as large as it is later in adolescence and young adulthood. Moreover, as we shall see, certain groups of males are believed to be at greater risk of developing an eating disorder.

Although eating disorders typically develop in males, as in females, during adolescence and young adulthood, some researchers have found a slightly later onset for males. For both, adolescence is normally a time of rebellion, experimentation, search for identity, and yearning for acceptance by peers. As a result, many of the variables that play into the development of eating disorders for females contribute to the occurrence in males.

THE DEVELOPMENT OF EATING DISORDERS IN MALES

The sociocultural influences that bombard girls and women in our society with images of ultrathin "waif" models, and encourage them to imitate such unrealistic body forms, are not as strong for boys and men. Appearance does not "define" men in quite the same way. Attributes such as power, money, and success are typically held in more esteem, providing young men with other outlets for achieving self-confidence. Yet boys entering puberty see appearance as important to their sexual appeal and popularity. In contrast to females, males are more dissatisfied with their upper bodies and usually more concerned about shape than weight. Media messages and social pressures have increased in recent years for young men to have broad shoulders, slim hips, "washboard" abdominal muscles, and an overall "cut" or "buff" appearance. A study of *Playgirl* centerfolds showed

that the males depicted there have become increasingly muscular over the last twenty-five years. Similarly, male toy action
figures have become more muscular over time; many of their
physiques far exceed the muscularity of the most robust human
bodybuilders. The trends are believed to reflect the increasing
social desirability of heightened muscle tone in men. Media ad-
vertising now targets younger men and promises them greater
sexual attractiveness and popularity in conjunction with a trim,
muscular body. Consequently, body dissatisfaction is growing in
a younger group of boys. Designer ads on television and in magazines are showing more and more of the male body, and it stands
to reason that young men in our society get the clear message
that appearance is vital to acceptance and desirability. Susceptible boys may resort to unhealthy measures in an attempt to
turn their bodies into society's male ideal and thereby attain a
feeling of accomplishment and well-being.

Males, like females, have been subjected to a shift in cultural
expectations of behavior. While success, power, and money are
still crucial, society has begun to look for more from males. In
the past, a man's primary role in the family was that of provider.
Today society also expects men to take a more emotionally active
role in relationships. It is an expectation that may be difficult for
those who were taught to hide their feelings, who learned that
"real men don't cry." Some boys and men find themselves confused about their emotions and how to express them. In addition, media images encourage rapid involvement in sexual behavior at ever younger ages. As with girls and young women,
these kinds of pressures cause some to turn to their bodies as
a way to demonstrate success, to flaunt or deny their sexuality,
and/or to deal with their feelings.

Beyond the societal influences that push young men to ma-
nipulate their weight and bodies, certain sports and occupations encourage males to restrict food intake. Examples are male

wrestlers, weight lifters, jockeys, flight attendants, models, and dancers. Men in the military have also been identified as a high-risk group because of the emphasis the armed forces place on weight control. Additionally, homosexuality and bisexuality may put some men at greater risk for eating disorders owing to the value that the gay male subculture places on thinness. However, the emaciated physiques of those stricken by AIDS may be moving the desirability of thinness to a healthier image.

Though not well studied, certain emotional features and personality characteristics seem to be associated with males who have eating disorders. Like females presenting with these illnesses, males often report feelings of depression and anxiety. They describe greater unhappiness with their bodies and more confusion about their emotions and physical sensations (such as hunger) than do males without eating disorders. Obsessive-compulsive behavior and obsessive-compulsive personality characteristics are quite common; the thoughts and behavior may or may not be food related. As discussed in Chapter 2, obsessions are unwanted thoughts that repeatedly enter a person's mind and cause anxiety. Compulsions are the behaviors that an individual feels required to engage in to decrease the anxiety caused by the obsessions. As with females, examples of obsessive-compulsive behaviors that are directly related to an eating disorder include constant calculation of calories and fat grams, frequent weighing, and compulsive exercising. For males, research shows that the compulsion to exercise excessively is especially powerful when compared to females.

At times, the obsessive-compulsive behaviors may be severe enough to warrant a diagnosis of obsessive-compulsive disorder and necessitate specific treatments designed for that illness. Young men with obsessive-compulsive personality characteristics are apt to be preoccupied with orderliness, rules, and details. They also tend to be perfectionistic. Together, these traits can produce a great deal of anxiety in males who cannot attain their unrealistically high standards. These individuals may take a long time to complete tasks, or they may not complete them at all because of continually attempting to improve on what they have done.

From a developmental perspective, adolescence is an emotionally turbulent time in which teens are searching for their own values, beliefs, opinions, and identity. This period is often characterized by rebelling against authority figures, clinging to peer norms, and wrestling with conflicts between societal, family, and peer beliefs. If the process proceeds as expected, teens eventually emerge with a clearer sense of self. Still, the process can go awry for males as well as females. An eating disorder can bring relief or divert attention from difficult issues by substituting a focus on weight, number of calories ingested, and amount of exercise performed.

As we pointed out earlier, no one knows for sure what role the family plays in the development of these illnesses. We do know that the context, or backdrop, in which an eating disorder develops is the family. Research has shown that males who report an adverse family background, in terms of negative parent-child interactions and negative parenting behavior, are at greater risk than other young men for developing an eating disorder. Our clinical experience has shown that the types of family dynamics that contribute to the development of an eating disorder are similar in the two sexes. Specifically, problems related to emotional separation, individuation, communication, and control are common. Individuation refers to a person's ability to establish a separate identity, including opinions, tastes, values, and goals that differ from those of the family of origin. In individuals who have successfully completed this necessary developmental task, an overlap may remain between opinions, values, and goals, but an independent, distinct sense of self has emerged which differs from that of the family. Family therapists frequently describe families who have a daughter with an eating disorder as "enmeshed," with members being emotionally overinvolved with one another. This phenomenon can occur with sons, as well. In contrast, family members can be emotionally alienated from one another or abusive in some way, which also interferes with growing up emotionally. These kinds of familial environments can also spawn eating disorders. For more information on the family dynamics associated with eating disorders, refer to Chapter 4.

With respect to the genetic influences on eating disorders, almost all research has been done with females. One study, however, found that anorexia tends to run in the families of males in much the same way that it does with females. This area of research obviously requires more investigation.

TREATMENT

The treatment principles that are effective for females with eating disorders are also effective for males. It is therefore crucial that treatment include the elements outlined in Chapter 5. In general, the therapeutic issues that must be addressed and resolved for recovery are similar in males and females. Certain psychological issues, however, are unique to males.

First, the personal and societal stigmas of an eating disorder are often worse for males because eating disorders are thought of by many as women's diseases. Thus, therapeutic work must be done with males to help them cope with this issue, particularly if they participate in a group setting in which the majority of patients are female. A men's group is often beneficial to avoid feelings of isolation, as is the inclusion of males on the patient's treatment team. Furthermore, the role of males in our society demands special attention in therapy because of the new emotional demands society currently places on them.

It may be difficult for boys and men who have not been encouraged to express themselves emotionally to handle these expectations. Like females, they are apt to need training in identification and communication of feelings. Even participating in psychotherapy, which is a "talking therapy," may be very difficult for some males. These sorts of obstacles must be dealt with early in treatment.

Finally, issues around sexuality must be discussed. Society has different sexual standards for men than it does for women. Like females recovering from anorexia, males with the illness must cope with the physical and emotional return of sexual feelings brought about by weight gain, which may be frightening. In contrast, some males with bulimia need to differentiate between appropriate and inappropriate sexual activity and learn how to control sexual and other impulses. Conflicts regarding sexual orientation may also need to be explored, as this issue is more common in males with eating disorders than in females. In summary, therapy must address these serious issues with an understanding of how males tend to view relationships, emotions, and sexual activity from both a collective and a personal vantage point.

In terms of medical problems, many of the physical complications that occur in females also affect males, although differences in the reproductive systems lead to associated concerns that are distinct for the sexes. Analogous to loss of the menstrual cycle in females, males with anorexia typically have low testosterone levels secondary to low weight. Sufficient weight gain usually corrects this problem.

GETTING WELL

In the past, it was erroneously believed that males did not fare as well in treatment as females. Today we know that they do respond as well, and that most of the factors that predict a successful outcome for females also predict success for males. In addition, males can do well in group settings where most of the patients are female. Both early detection and prompt treatment of eating disorders in males are essential for a favorable prognosis, just as they are in females. As with females with these illnesses, males can and do recover when the appropriate treatment is completed.

Selected Bibliography

Andersen, A. E. (1990). *Males with eating disorders.* New York: Brunner/Mazel.

Andersen, A. E. (1995). Eating disorders in males. In K. D. Brownell & C. G. Fairburn (Eds.), *Eating disorders and obesity: A comprehensive handbook* (pp. 177–182). New York: Guilford Press.

Andersen, A. E. (1999). Gender-related aspects of eating disorders: A guide to practice. *Journal of Gender-Specific Medicine, 2,* 47–54.

Andersen, A. E., Cohn, L., & Holbrook, T. (2000). *Making Weight: Healing Men's Conflicts with Food, Weight and Shape.* Carlsbad, California: Gurze Books.

Andersen, A. E., & Holman, J. E. (1997). Males with eating disorders: Challenges for treatment and research. *Psychopharmacology Bulletin, 33,* 391–397.

Braun, D. L., Sunday, S. R., Huang, A., & Halmi, K. A. (1999). More males seek treatment for eating disorders. *International Journal of Eating Disorders, 25,* 415–424.

Bryant-Waugh, R., & Lask, B. (1995). Childhood onset of eating disorders. In K. D. Brownell and C. G. Fairburn (Eds.), *Eating disorders and obesity: A comprehensive handbook* (pp. 183–187). New York: Guilford Press.

Carlat, D. J., Camargo, C. A., Jr., & Herzog, D. B. (1997). Eating disorders in males: A report on 135 patients. *American Journal of Psychiatry, 154,* 1127–1132.

Crisp, A. H., Burns, T., & Bhat, A. V. (1986). Primary anorexia in the male and female: A comparison of clinical features and prognosis. *British Journal of Medical Psychology, 59 (Pt. 2),* 123–132.

Farrow, J. A. (1992). The adolescent male with an eating disorder. *Pediatric Annals, 21,* 769–774.

Geist, R., Heinmaa, M., Katzman, D., & Stephens, D. (1999). A comparison of male and female adolescents referred to an eating disorder program. *Canadian Journal of Psychiatry, 44,* 374–378.

Herzog, D. B., Bradburn, I. S., & Newman, K. (1990). Sexuality in males with eating disorders. In A. Andersen (Ed.), *Males with eating disorders* (pp. 40–53). New York: Brunner/Mazel.

Kakaiya, D., & Mowafy, M. (2001). Media now targeting young men. *Eating Disorders Review, 12,* 1.

Keel, P. K., Klump, K. L., Leon, G. R., & Fulkerson, J. A. (1998). Disordered eating in adolescent males from a school-based sample. *International Journal of Eating Disorders, 23,* 125–132.

Kinzl, J. F., Mangweth, B., Traweger, C. M., & Biebl, W. (1997). Eating-disordered behavior in males: The impact of adverse childhood experiences. *International Journal of Eating Disorders, 22,* 131–138.

Leit, R. A., Pope, H. J., Jr., & Gray, J. J. (2001). Cultural expectations of muscularity in men: The evolution of Playgirl centerfolds. *International Journal of Eating Disorders, 29,* 90–93.

Margo, J. L. (1987). Anorexia nervosa in males: A comparison with female patients. *British Journal of Psychiatry, 151,* 80–83.

McNulty, P. A. (1997). Prevalence and contributing factors of eating disorder behaviors in active duty Navy men. *Military Medicine, 162,* 753–758.

Mickalide, A. D. (1990). Sociocultural factors influencing weight among males. In A. Andersen (Ed.), *Males with eating disorders* (pp. 30–39). New York: Brunner/Mazel.

Minuchin S., Rosman, B. L., & Baker, L. (1978). *Psychosomatic families: Anorexia nervosa in context.* Cambridge, Massachusetts: Harvard University Press.

O'Dea, J. A., & Abraham, S. (1999). Onset of disordered eating attitudes and behaviors in early adolescence: Interplay of pubertal status, gender, weight, and age. *Adolescence, 34,* 671–679.

Pope, H. G., Jr., Olivardia, R., Gruber, A., & Borowiecki, J. (1999). Evolving ideals of male body image as seen through action toys. *International Journal of Eating Disorders, 26,* 65–72.

Selvini-Palazzoli, M. (1974). *Self starvation.* New York: Jason Aronson.

Sharp, C. W., Clark, S. A., Dunan, J. R., Blackwood, D. H., & Shapiro, C. M. (1994). Clinical presentation of anorexia nervosa in males: 24 new cases. *International Journal of Eating Disorders, 15,* 125–134.

Strober, M., Freeman, R., Lampert, C., Diamond, J., & Kaye, W. (2001). Males with anorexia nervosa: A controlled study of eating disorders in first-degree relatives. *International Journal of Eating Disorders, 29,* 263–269.

Tomova, A., & Kumanov, P. (1999). Sex differences and similarities of hormonal alterations in patients with anorexia nervosa. *Andrologia, 31,* 143–147.

Touyz, S. W., Kopec-Schrader, E. M., & Beumont, P. J. (1993). Anorexia nervosa in males: A report of 12 cases. *Australian and New Zealand Journal of Psychiatry, 27,* 512–517.

Vandereycken, W., & Van den Broucke, S. (1984). Anorexia nervosa in males: A comparative study of 107 cases reported in the literature (1970 to 1980). *Acta Psychiatrica Scandinavica, 70,* 447–454.

Woodside, D. B., & Kaplan, A. S. (1994). Day hospital treatment in males with eating disorders-response and comparison to females. *Journal of Psychosomatic Research, 38,* 471–475.

eight

How Does a Nonspecialist Assess, Treat, and Refer Someone with an Eating Disorder?

Assessment and treatment of people with eating disorders can be challenging for even the most seasoned eating disorders specialists. When professionals whose expertise is in a different area are confronted with these difficult cases, they can become frustrated, overwhelmed, and even frightened. Over years of practice we have compiled a set of guidelines for physicians, mental health professionals, and nutritionists who do not specialize in the treatment of eating disorders but who want to know what to do if they suspect that an individual presenting for evaluation and/or treatment has an eating disorder. These guidelines are meant to serve only as a general reference for common therapeutic interactions; it would be impossible to address every scenario the clinician might encounter.

The evaluation of those who have eating disorders requires inquiry into the psychological features of the illnesses as well as the associated physical symptoms. Consequently, health care professionals, regardless of their discipline, need to be familiar with both areas of inquiry. The following sections provide guidelines for the nonspecialist health care professional on how to assess a patient for an eating disorder and facilitate treatment when necessary.

PHYSICIANS

Assessment For physicians, knowledge of the physical symptoms specifically associated with anorexia and bulimia is critical. It is often the medical problems, such as weight loss, syncope, or dizziness that initially bring the patient to the doctor's office. In addition, it is important for all physicians to be familiar with the diagnostic criteria for these illnesses, as stipulated by the American Psychiatric Association in the fourth edition of the *Diagnostic and Statistical Manual of Mental Disorders* (or DSM-IV). Familiarity with these criteria serves as a general guide when considering the possibility of an eating disorder. In order to conduct a more thorough evaluation, however, knowledge of the warning signs and symptoms is needed. A review of Chapter 2 of this book will assist the physician in recognizing the physical symptoms, diagnostic criteria, and warning signs of anorexia and bulimia. We also recommend asking the following key questions when evaluating a patient who might have an eating disorder:

How do you see your body?
How do you feel about the way you look?
What do you think would be an ideal weight for you?
Are you dieting?
Do you count calories or fat grams?
How often do you exercise and for what length of time?
When was your last menstrual period?
How often do you weigh yourself?
Do you ever vomit after eating?
Do you ever take laxatives or syrup of ipecac?
Do you ever use diet pills, herbal teas, or diuretics?

Do you ever take Mini-Thins or fat-burner pills?
Do you ever use enemas?

Not only do physicians need to know what type of questions to ask patients they suspect might have an eating disorder, but they must also anticipate incriminating questions patients presenting at normal, near normal, or low weight may ask them. The questions asked could reflect the eating disordered behaviors in which these patients engage:

Would you prescribe diet pills for me?
Would you recommend a liquid diet?
Would you recommend a low-fat diet?
Would you recommend a vegetarian diet?
Would you prescribe diuretics for the bloating I get just before
    my period?
What can I take for constipation?
Would you please not tell my parents how much weight I have
    lost?
Would you refer me to a plastic surgeon for liposuction?

Because of the many potentially serious medical complications, as well as the denial and secretive behaviors involved in eating disorders, laboratory and medical evaluation can provide highly significant information. The two basic types of assessments are a standard evaluation and an evaluation prompted by special clinical circumstances. The physician can use abnormal test results to convince the patient and her family of the need for treatment. Conversely, normal test results can lead physicians, patients, and families to a false sense of security. We have known patients who were very ill, yet continued to have normal laboratory reports and other medical test results. Test results can change quickly, however, and patients with these illnesses can

STANDARD LABORATORY AND MEDICAL
ASSESSMENTS FOR PATIENTS WITH
EATING DISORDERS

- Complete metabolic profile: albumin, alkaline phosphatase, aspartate aminotransference (AST), blood urea nitrogen (BUN), calcium, carbon dioxide, chloride, creatinine, globulin, glucose, potassium, sodium, total bilirubin, and total protein
- Complete blood count (CBC)
- Urinalysis (UA)
- Serum magnesium
- Thyroid screen (T3, T4, TSH)
- Electrocardiogram (ECG)

(lists on this and facing page adapted from the American Psychiatric Association, 2000, and Powers, 2000)

die suddenly and without warning. Thus, laboratory studies constitute only part of the evaluation process.

Facilitating Treatment The physician is obviously the member of the multidisciplinary treatment team who assesses and treats any medical complications that result from the eating disorder. It is crucial that the physician in this role be aware of the associated medical conditions that require prompt hospitalization. It is beyond the scope of this book to describe either the treatment of such complications or comorbid chronic medical conditions; therefore, references that the physician will find useful are listed in Appendix B.

In addition to assessing and treating medical problems, the physician is often the person who carries the burden of facilitat-

SPECIAL LABORATORY AND MEDICAL
ASSESSMENTS FOR PATIENTS WITH EATING
DISORDERS (IBW = IDEAL BODY WEIGHT)

- If 15% or more <IBW: chest X-ray, complement 3 (C3), 24-hour creatinine clearance, uric acid
- If 20% or more <IBW and/or any neurological sign: brain magnetic resistance imaging (MRI) and computerized tomography (CT)
- If 20% or more <IBW and/or indication of mitral valve prolapse: echocardiogram
- If 30% or more <IBW: skin testing for immune functioning
- If underweight (15% <IBW) for more than six months, to assess for osteopenia and osteoporosis: dual-energy X-ray absorptiometry (DEXA), estradiol level in females, testosterone level in males
- If suspect recurrent or persistent vomiting: serum amylase level
- If suspect fluid loading: specific gravity or serum aldosterone level
- If persistent amenorrhea at a normal weight: luteinizing hormone (LH) and follicle-stimulating hormone (FSH)

ing psychiatric treatment for a reluctant patient and distraught family. If you are the doctor in such a position, your first step should be to associate yourself with a group of eating disorder specialists with whom you feel comfortable working. If you are unaware of specialists in your area, ask trusted medical colleagues or the Academy for Eating Disorders, the National Eating Disorders Association, and/or the Eating Disorders Referral and

CONDITIONS INDICATING NEED FOR
MEDICAL HOSPITALIZATION

Anorexia

- Hypophosphatemia
- Bone marrow failure
- Cardiac problems
- Shock

Bulimia

- Severe hypovolemia
- Cardiac arrhythmias
- Symtomatic electrolyte disturbances
- Significant gastrointestinal bleeding

Information Center (see Appendix A) for a referral. If there are no specialists in your area, locate the nearest team to whom you can refer patients for evaluation. The eating disorder specialists can assess the severity of the situation and recommend the best course of treatment with whatever resources are available.

When an eating disorder is suspected, rule out any medical etiology, treat the medical complications, then refer the patient to the eating disorder specialists as soon as possible. The earlier a diagnosis is made and multidisciplinary treatment initiated, the more favorable the prognosis. Be aware that patients may attempt to "bargain" their way out of psychiatric treatment by promising to gain weight, eat better, stop vomiting, and so forth. They often plead with their doctors and families to give them another chance to change. It is not unusual for patients to minimize or deny the severity of their disorders. Therefore, be firm with your recommendation: the longer it takes for the patient to receive psychiatric treatment, the more likely it is that she will deteriorate both physically and psychologically. In addition, treatment becomes more difficult as the attitudes and behaviors become more indelibly ingrained and the person is consumed both physically and psychologically by the eating disorder. On the other hand, watch for the superficially compliant patient who readily agrees to follow all instructions but manifests no change. If this situation occurs, speak with the individual psychotherapist about developing a contingency plan to facilitate behavioral change.

When it comes to treatment, the physician's wholehearted support of the mental health professionals on the team is paramount. Specifically, it is important that the doctor rely on and support the mental health professionals in their efforts to solve the underlying psychological problems that have generated the physical symptoms. Recognizing that eating disorders are psychiatric illnesses with physical ramifications allows the physician to insist that the patient and her family seek and actively participate in psychological treatment. If patient and/or family resistance is interfering with recommended care, the physician can work with those involved to keep treatment from being disrupted. He or she is in a powerful position to help patients and their families understand that psychiatric care is integral to recovery.

When medical information needs to be transmitted to the rest of the treatment team, communicate with the individual therapist or the nutritionist. It is vital that the team remain in close contact and exchange all pertinent information. Team members can thereby make unanimous, informed decisions regarding treatment. Discuss any questions or concerns you may have as soon as possible with the treatment team. Retaining close contact will preempt misunderstandings and attempts by the patient and/or her family to split the team.

Finally, see the patient as infrequently as is medically feasible, and allow only the nutritionist to weigh the patient. The nutritionist can report the weight back to you if you wish. Weighing in the physician's office can be traumatic for someone with an eating disorder. Remember that the patient focuses on her body and weight as a way of distracting herself from underlying psychological problems. The nutritionist who specializes in eating disorders has expertise in handling the psychological issues that arise when the patient is weighed, and the experience can turn into a therapeutic encounter instead of a traumatic event. Overinvolvement of the physician in the nonmedical, weight-related issues supports the erroneous notion that eating disorders are of physical origin. Understandably, it is easier for the patient and her family to believe that there is an underlying medical problem rather than face psychological and possible family disturbance. The physician is in an ideal position to dispel that myth.

DENTISTS

It is known that dental and throat problems are common medical complications associated with bulimia. For this reason, it is not unusual for the bulimic's dentist to be the first person to suspect her illness. Cavities, enamel erosion, persistent throat irritation, and chronic hoarseness can result from frequent vomiting. These symptoms may also be observed in the anorexic who is purging by means of self-induced vomiting. If the patient is not in treatment for an eating disorder, she may not admit to disordered eating, and she may make excuses for any physical problems on which the dentist comments. It is important, then, that the dentist be familiar with the diagnostic criteria for these illnesses as stipulated by the American Psychiatric Association in the DSM-IV. The dentist also needs to know the warning signs and symptoms. A review of chapter 2 of this book will assist the dentist in recognizing the physical symptoms, diagnostic criteria, and warning signs of anorexia and bulimia. For more detailed information on the dental complications of eating disorders, consult the dentistry section of *Medical Issues and the Eating Disorders: The Interface.*

To recapitulate part of what was outlined in the section for physicians, if you as a dentist suspect that one of your patients has an eating disorder, inform her of your concerns in a supportive fashion, giving her the reasons for your suspicions. If she is a minor, you will also have to meet with her family to express your concerns, preferably with the patient present. Next, refer her for an eating disorder evaluation. To make this step easier, associate yourself with a group of specialists with whom you feel comfortable working. Some eating disorder treatment teams even include a dentist as part of their health care staff. If you do not know of any specialists in your area, seek information from trusted colleagues or the Academy for Eating Disorders, National Eating Disorders Association, and/or the Eating Disorder Referral and Information Center. If there are no specialists in your area, identify the nearest team to whom you can refer patients for evaluation. The eating disorder specialists can then assess the severity of the situation and recommend the best course of treatment with the available resources.

A dentist who understands the complexity of eating disorders as well as their psychiatric origin is a valuable team member. With respect to treatment, he or she can offer instructions on preventive care to avoid dental caries and enamel erosion caused by acidic contact. He or she can also provide essential education about all the dental dangers of vomiting. The ability to be warm and supportive is important because of the shame associated with purging behavior. The anorexic or bulimic is more likely to engage in regular dental care if she knows that her dentist will be nonjudgmental and caring. For an in-depth discussion of how to treat the dental complications brought about by regular, self-induced vomiting, see the chapter on dentistry in *Medical Issues and the Eating Disorders.*

MENTAL HEALTH PROFESSIONALS

Assessment Evaluation of someone with a suspected or known eating disorder has many similarities to other mental health evaluations, but also important differences. For a comprehensive evaluation, several assessments must take place—including a psychosocial interview, a nutritional assessment, and a medical examination. A physician is oftentimes the referring party and the patient's medical status is already known. At other times it will fall to the mental health professional to refer the patient for a medical evaluation. In either case, we recommend that all assessments take place within an abbreviated time frame, as close scheduling allows maximum and immediate communication of information among treatment team members. Explain ahead of time to the patient and her family that unrestricted communication of information among team members is necessary in order to develop and implement an individualized treatment plan. It is recommended that you have all parties sign a release of information to this effect.

Because of the ego-syntonic nature of anorexia and the shame and embarrassment associated with bulimia, many patients are resistant to undergoing an eating disorder evaluation. They may deny problems, minimize them, or leave out important information. We therefore recommend gathering data from as many different sources as possible. Ideally, the evaluation would comprise an individual interview with the identified patient, a conjoint family interview (with the patient present), and any other relevant information obtained from the patient's physician, school, and other involved parties. If indicated, psychological testing and/or a psychiatric consultation may be scheduled after the initial evaluation.

A thorough assessment is the foundation of a viable, individualized treatment plan. Careful attention must be given to obtaining information on historical and current physical status, eating disorder history and severity, associated psychiatric disturbances, developmental history, physical and sexual trauma history, and family background including an assessment of family dynamics. Concomitant and historical substance abuse should be evaluated; if substance abuse is a primary problem, a proper referral should be made and the abuse treated before the eating disorder is addressed. It is impossible to access the underlying psychological issues when substance use is masking feelings and altering cognitive experience. If the eating disorder is severe, however, simultaneous treatment may be necessary, usually on an inpatient basis.

When taking the eating disorder history, you will want to know the specifics of food restriction, such as how many calories and fat grams the patient eats per day, as well as the presence or absence of binge eating. Ask the patient to give you a concrete example of a binge to see if it meets the clinical definition given in the DSM-IV. An anorexic may tell you that she binges, but her idea of a binge may be two low-calorie, fat-free cookies, which certainly does not fit the clinical definition. It is important to inquire into the sense of control the person feels when she "binges." Is she capable of stopping herself? Loss of control over binge eating is a defining characteristic of bulimia and of the binge eating/purging type of anorexia. Ask as well about any changes in her patterns of eating over time. Many people with an eating disorder will cycle through different patterns, some moving back and forth between restricting type anorexia and binge eating/purging type anorexia or bulimia.

AREAS OF INQUIRY IN THE
PSYCHOSOCIAL EVALUATION

Medical History
- Physical
- Laboratory tests
- Gynecological

Eating Disorder History
- Eating attitudes and patterns
- Purging behavior
- Diet aids
- Exercise patterns
- Body image
- Cosmetic surgery

Comorbid Psychiatric Problems
- Depression
- Anxiety
- Obsessive-compulsive features
- Substance abuse

Trauma History
- Physical abuse
- Sexual abuse
- Emotional abuse
- Neglect

Family History and Dynamics
- Eating attitudes and patterns
- Roles and relationships
- Medical history
- Psychiatric history

Social and Occupational History
- Interpersonal relationships
- Social life
- Education
- Occupation

In your investigation of purging behavior and diet aids, question the patient closely about self-induced vomiting as well as the use of laxatives, emetics, herbal teas, and diet pills. Inquire about substances with ephedrine or "ma huang" (Mini-Thins, Dexatrim, Xenadrine), as these substances can be lethal when abused. Assess whether the patient uses substances such as No-Doze or asthma inhalants to increase her heartrate, in the belief that doing so will help her burn calories. When evaluating self-induced vomiting, be sure to ask how the patient induces vomiting: does she use her finger, or does she engage in a more dangerous practice such as using a spoon or toothbrush? For many who purge, simply bending over a toilet becomes a conditioned response, so that other means of induction are not necessary. In addition, it is worthwhile to ask about the use of any "health products for weight control"; many young girls believe that if they buy one of the popular diet aids available in a health food store, or if a product is labeled "all natural," then it must be healthy.

Your inquiry into exercise patterns should include the frequency, duration, and time of day or night that the person exercises, in addition to the type of exercise. It sheds light on the severity of an individual's illness if you discover that she gets up in the middle of the night to exercise so that she is not just "lying there getting fat." Assessing body image should include questions about the person's desired weight, how she views her body, and any special areas of body dissatisfaction. An inexperienced professional may be confused when an anorexic says that she does not see herself as fat, but thinks she looks fine. It is important to understand that seeing herself as "fine" when she is emaciated qualifies her body image as distorted.

Assessment of common comorbid conditions includes questions about depression, anxiety, obsessive-compulsive behavior, and substance abuse. Any or all of these problems may justify additional diagnoses and warrant consideration for hospitalization or consultation with a psychiatrist for pharmacotherapy. The obsessive-compulsive behavior may or may not be eating disorder related. Questions you might ask to assess food-related obsessions include, "What percentage of the time do you think about food?" and "What percentage of the time do you think about calories or fat grams?" Compulsive eating disordered behavior may be evidenced by the patient's frequency of exercise or weighing. It may also be seen in how she eats, cutting her food into tiny pieces or counting every bite. To reiterate, if substance abuse or dependence is found to be a primary problem, it must be addressed before the eating disorder can be successfully treated. If the substance abuse is secondary to the eating disorder, or in the case of a severe eating disorder and comorbid substance abuse, concomitant treatment is recommended.

When taking a trauma history, it is important to delineate the time frame surrounding the trauma and the onset of the eating disorder, for there is frequently a connection. If a history of trauma is revealed, one should ask about dissociative symptoms, which may be isolated symptoms or may warrant an additional diagnosis. Presence of a trauma history complicates treatment in that the individual therapist needs to assess the patient's tolerance for insight-oriented psychotherapy and her ability to contain any dissociative symptomatology. If dissociative symptoms are severe, treatment of the dissociative disorder may be required prior to successful treatment of the eating disorder. When the conditions coexist, the optimal treatment is in a program with specialized expertise in both areas, where care can be coordinated and titrated according to each patient's needs.

Upon assessment, the role of family dynamics in the development and maintenance of an eating disorder becomes apparent. Evaluation of family eating attitudes and patterns, as well as examination of family roles and relationships, can be particularly enlightening. Many families are focused on appearance with a family history of dieting, exercise, eating disorders, and preoccupation with weight (see Chapter 4 for a more thorough explanation). Issues having to do with separation and individuation often come up, as manifested by enmeshment or disengagement among family members. It is essential that you pass on any observations of this nature to the designated family therapist. As with any psychosocial evaluation, family medical and psychiatric history should also be obtained.

The last portion of the psychosocial evaluation includes the patient's social and occupational history. Individuals who have eating disorders are usually achievement oriented and do well educationally and occupationally until the eating disorder impairs their functioning. Some individuals continue doing remarkably well, even when you would expect their eating disorder to have prevented them from doing so. Difficulties with interpersonal relationships are characteristic of this patient population; relationships are therefore a major focus of treatment. Evaluation of friendships, romantic partners or lack thereof, and overall social functioning is necessary so that interpersonal problems can be dealt with directly.

Structured Interview Forms and Eating Disorder Questionnaires Structured interview forms and eating disorder questionnaires are helpful in assisting the clinician to evaluate attitudes, behaviors, and beliefs associated with eating disorders. Information obtained in this manner must be combined, however, with the other sources of information described above. Furthermore, if the clinician chooses to use structured forms as part of the assessment, he or she must be familiar with the purposes, strengths, and limitations of any interview form or questionnaire chosen. Below are selected eating disorders structured interview forms and questionnaires:

Bulimia Test-Revised (BULIT-R)
Children's Eating Attitudes Test (ChEAT)
Clinical Eating Disorder Rating Instrument (CEDRI)
Eating Attitudes Test (EAT)
Eating Disorders Examination (EDE)
Eating Disorders Inventory-2 (EDI-2)
Interview for Diagnosis of Eating Disorders (IDED)
Kids' Eating Disorders Survey (KEDS)
Structured Interview for Anorexia and Bulimia (SIAB)

TO REFER OR NOT TO REFER?

Whether or not to refer a patient with an eating disorder to someone who specializes in the field is a complicated question. The answer is dependent on several factors: (1) your relationship with the patient, (2) the severity of the eating disorder, (3) your comfort level and attitude, (4) the availability of specialists, and (5) managed care considerations.

The first factor has to do with the quality of your relationship with the patient. If you have already established rapport and a strong therapeutic alliance with her, it may be ill advised to refer to someone else. As most clinicians recognize, the therapeutic relationship is the foundation for change and is, according to the psychotherapy literature, one of the most important contributing variables for change. It is within the context of your relationship that the patient will mature developmentally, resolve her identity issues, and ultimately let go of her eating disorder. If, however, the alliance is not firmly grounded, or if you have seen the patient infrequently, referral may be indicated. It may also be advisable to refer if your first encounter with the patient has been for an evaluation.

The severity of an eating disorder is paramount when deciding whether or not to refer a patient. Someone with a life-threatening illness would probably be best served by an eating disorder specialist who is associated with a multidisciplinary team. If the patient's symptoms are acute (very low weight, rapid weight loss, out-of-control purging, or an electrolyte imbalance), referral to a specialist who could promptly engage a team is advisable. On the other hand, if the patient's disorder is not so severe, you may feel comfortable continuing treatment yourself. As with all psychotherapy, respecting your bounds of competence is necessary; if an individual you are treating does not respond favorably or worsens, referral to a specialist might be prudent. Consultation with an expert on eating disorders could help you decide whether or not referral is warranted.

Another variable that will affect your decision about referral is your own comfort level with, and attitude toward, this patient population. As mentioned earlier, this group of patients can be frightening to work with because of their potentially life-threatening illnesses. Many therapists are uneasy treating this population, especially if their experience in treatment of eating disorders is limited. It should be noted that any biases or negative attitudes that one might have toward those with eating disorders will likely impede the therapist's ability to facilitate change. Furthermore, this population is known to elicit strong countertransference in therapists. The therapist must therefore evaluate his or her feelings and decide if the challenges of treatment can be withstood.

Referral may also be based on the availability of specialists in your area. If no one in your locale has expertise in the field and the patient does not wish to go elsewhere, your options are limited. If you decide to implement treatment, the guidelines in the following section will assist you in providing the best care possible. If the patient is suffering from a severe eating disorder, has serious medical problems, or is on the brink of hospitalization, it may be imperative that she see an eating disorder specialist. Sometimes this circumstance mandates that the patient travel to receive adequate treatment.

Finally, managed care has greatly impacted the field of eating disorders to the extent that many plans refuse to cover any treatment whatsoever. The insurance companies that do cover eating disorders often impose limitations, such as select providers, restricted hospitalization benefits, and limited outpatient visits. These and other obstacles have made it financially difficult or impossible for many patients to procure the long-term, comprehensive treatment that is required for them to return to healthy, productive lives. If you encounter this type of problem, encourage the holder of the insurance policy to persuade his or her employer (or whoever pays the premiums) to lobby the insurance company to approve needed treatment. It may be possible to transfer dollars allocated for "medical benefits" to "psychiatric benefits" to obtain the needed coverage. Many of our own patients and their families have been quite successful with this aggressive approach. It may also be helpful to contact the state insurance commissioner or enlist the support of eating disorder advocacy groups (see the list in Appendix A). You can review Margo Maine's arguments and strategies in Chapter 5, and identify possible educational and governmental resources.

Treatment If you do decide to treat someone with an eating disorder, we recommend that you consult with an eating disorder specialist, if possible. A consultation will assist you in determining the severity of the problem and alert you to any pressing psychological or medical concerns. For example, a patient who agrees to discontinue laxative use may consequently suffer from fluid retention, or rebound edema. The patient is likely to erroneously interpret the swelling as "fat" and become frightened. Often she will start taking laxatives again in an attempt to reduce the swelling or, in her mind, "lose the fat." Consultation with an eating disorder specialist who could predict the rebound edema and guide you in how to handle it therapeutically could ward off such a problem.

The preceding example also illustrates the need for inexperienced therapists to work under supervision with this patient population. Continued supervision can alleviate a new therapist's anxieties as well as ensure the best of care for the patient. Participation in educational conferences and workshops is also recommended to increase the therapist's knowledge and confidence.

Effective treatment of eating disorders requires multidisciplinary intervention. It is therefore crucial to form a team of experts if you choose to treat these individuals. Such a team should include, at a minimum, the individual therapist, plus a nutritionist, family therapist, and physician. Others (medical specialists, athletic coaches, teachers) may be included as therapeutically indicated. Just as it is important for physicians to find specialists with whom they are comfortable working, it is necessary for individual therapists to build treatment teams composed of professionals with whom they are comfortable as well. Regular communication among all team members is essential to avoid splitting and to make certain that everyone is moving in the same direction with the same goals. It is often necessary for certain team members (usually the individual therapist and nutritionist) to communicate with one another after each session, especially when hospitalization is being considered. The individual therapist serves as head of the team, since individual psychotherapy is the cornerstone of treatment. It is that person's responsibility to ensure that each component of treatment is implemented as initially recommended.

It is essential to be able to recognize when hospitalization is indicated. The reasons may be medical, psychiatric, or a combination of the two (see Chapter 5). Working in concert with a multidisciplinary team will give you the assurance that medical complications can be caught early and appropriate care provided. We have also noted from our experience that some life-threatening eating disorder behaviors, self-harm behaviors, and/or potentially dangerous feelings of hopelessness are disclosed to certain members of the team but not to others. For example, a patient may reveal thoughts of suicide to the nutritionist but not to the therapist. Again, careful communication among team members will ensure that any concerns are conveyed to all members. With this approach, problems can be addressed adequately and in a timely fashion.

NUTRITIONISTS

As the person who most directly deals with food issues, the nutritionist has a special role in assessment and treatment of eating disorders. Since food is both loved and hated by those with eating disorders, the patient is likely to have strong feelings about seeing the nutritionist, some of which may be positive and some of which may be negative. The dietician working with eating disordered patients needs to understand the complexity and nature of eating disorders. He or she must be able to build a trusting relationship with the patient—one that is born of caring, warmth, and support. The nutritionist will need to be firm at times, particularly when the patient's immediate health is at stake. The ability to know when to back off from an issue, strongly confront an issue, or refer a psychological issue back to the individual psychotherapist is vital. Nutritional counseling is much more than straightforward education about nutrition; it requires the dietician to understand the psychological dynamics of eating disorders and to be flexible within the therapeutic relationship.

An overview of nutritional assessment and counseling is provided below. For a comprehensive review of the details involved, as well as detailed aspects of the nutritionist-patient relationship, see the references cited at the end of this chapter.

Nutrition Assessment The nutrition evaluation should be comprehensive and include height, current weight, weight changes over time, body fat and muscle analysis, percentage of weight deviation from the norm, ideal body-weight calculation, and menstrual cycle history. Detailed information should be gathered on eating patterns, including consumption of calories, fat, and other nutrients; diet history; and sample dietary intake over the course of a twenty-four-hour period. Sport and exercise history is important as are patient beliefs about food, weight, and hunger. Inquire about obsessions with food, weight, and body image, including the severity of the obsessions and any accompanying compulsions. Evaluation of food fears is essential as well. Evaluate any eating disordered behaviors such as bingeing, purging, and use of dietary aids. Ask the patient about her sources of nutritional information, so that you will be familiar with her knowledge base and can use it therapeutically, or explain why the source is not reliable. Review the sections of this chapter for physicians and mental health professionals for specific questions to ask regarding eating disordered behavior.

Information gathered in the assessment will enable the nutritionist to calculate ideal body weight (IBW) for low-weight patients and set an appropriate weight range. Several different means are used by professionals to determine IBW. The goal is to set a weight range that allows for healthy functioning of the reproductive system (menstruation, in females) and the rest of the body. The Robinson formula is often used for this purpose:

> For an adult female or a postmenarchal adolescent female with an average body frame, allow 100 pounds for 5 feet of height and add 5 pounds for every inch thereafter. For small-framed women and girls, subtract 10 percent of that result; for large-framed women, add 10 percent.
>
> For adult males with an average build, allow 106 pounds for 5 feet of height and add 6 pounds for every inch thereafter. Add or subtract 10 percent based on larger or smaller body frames, respectively, as with females.

Once IBW has been calculated, a five-pound target weight range should be set with the number resulting from your calculations in the middle of the range. Keep in mind, however, that these formulas are to be used as general guidelines only. The patient's weight history, menstrual history, familial weight history, and other factors may alter your determination of an appropriate weight range. For adolescents up to age twenty, it is recommended that growth charts be utilized as an aid in determining proper weight, along with weight history, menstrual history (if applicable), and other factors. In addition, some treatment teams use estradiol levels to determine if the patient's weight range is sufficient to allow menstruation to occur. Estradiol levels can be misleading, though, as they represent only one component of total estrogen levels at a given point in time. Pelvic ultrasounds can be used to remedy these difficulties, as they reflect endocrine and nutrition status for two months prior to testing.

For patients in need of weight gain, a projection system should be used in which the patient is required to gain approximately one to two pounds per week in outpatient treatment until she reaches her target weight range. This approach is intended to ensure that the patient is on track to reaching normal body weight at a medically feasible rate. If the patient is unwilling or unable to comply, inpatient treatment may become necessary. During the refeeding process, work with the physician to carefully monitor the patient for the following signs of refeeding syndrome: hypokalemia, cardiac arrhythmias, sudden decrease in potassium and/or magnesium, sudden and sometimes severe hypophosphatemia, glucose intolerance, and gastrointestinal dysfunction. Inform the patient that water retention is common during refeeding, so that she does not interpret edema as fat. Be prepared to discuss this issue repeatedly during the refeeding process. Review the box enumerating "Conditions Indicating Need for Medical Hospitalization" in the physician's portion of this chapter and see Chapter 5 for additional circumstances that may warrant inpatient treatment.

Nutritional Counseling At times, a patient and her family will agree that the patient needs to see a nutritionist but they refuse to believe that other treatment is necessary. This attitude indicates that they do not acknowledge the deeper problems that cause the symptoms. It is imperative that you insist on working with a multidisciplinary team. As previously discussed, having a nutritionist work with the patient on food and body issues will free the individual therapist and the patient to discover and resolve the psychological conflicts that have driven the symptoms. The role of the nutritionist is to provide nutritional support, education, and guidance, as well as assist the medical staff in monitoring vital signs, laboratory results, and other physical symptoms of malnutrition. Again, it is important to have an understanding of the psychological issues underlying eating disorders and to be psychologically minded, as emotional issues will certainly surface during nutrition counseling. Be in tune with the patient and her feelings associated with food behavior; when the patient identifies these emotions in sessions, you can recommend that she explore them further in individual psychotherapy. In this way, the nutritionist and individual psychotherapist work together in an effort to help the patient separate emotions from food. The nutritionist focuses more on the food and weight aspects of the disorder, while the psychotherapist focuses more on the emotions and cognitions.

The nutritionist must be cognizant of the ways in which an individual will attempt to hold on to her eating disorder, particularly when it comes to weight. Some patients who are on a weight gain protocol will resist by trying to artificially increase their weight by fluid loading prior to weighing, and/or by hiding weights, heavy change, or other objects on their bodies or in their clothes. Of course, for those on a weight-projection system, a time eventually comes when they cannot "pad" their weight sufficiently to meet the projection. For patients suspected of fluid loading, laboratory tests (specific gravity, serum aldosterone) can be ordered to help determine if that is the case. Suspicions about these sorts of self-destructive, manipulative behaviors must be confronted and team members notified immediately.

For more information on nutritional rehabilitation, see Chapter 5 of the book, *Eating Disorders: Nutrition Therapy in the Recovery Process*, and the American Dietetic Association's 2001 position paper on the nutritionist's role in the treatment of eating disorders.

In conclusion, let us reiterate that it is important for the nutritionist who is treating an individual with an eating disorder to have specialized training in the field or to be supervised by an experienced nutritionist. If you are having difficulty locating an experienced nutritionist in your area, contact the American Dietetic Association, the Academy for Eating Disorders, and/or the National Eating Disorders Association for references. Telephone numbers and addresses for these organizations are located in Appendix A.

Selected Bibliography

American Dietetic Association. (2001). Position of the American Dietetic Association: Nutrition intervention in the treatment of anorexia nervosa, bulimia nervosa, and eating disorders not otherwise specified (EDNOS). *Journal of the American Dietetic Association, 101,* 810–819.

American Psychiatric Association. (1994). *Diagnostic and statistical manual of mental disorders* (4th Ed.). Washington, D.C.: Author.

American Psychiatric Association Work Group on Eating Disorders. (2000). Practice guideline for the treatment of patients with eating disorders (Rev.). *American Journal of Psychiatry, 157 (Suppl. 1),* 1–39.

Beutler, L. E., Crago, M., & Arizmendi, T. G. (1986). Therapist variables in psychotherapy process and outcome. In S. L. Garfield and A. E. Bergin (Eds.), *Handbook of psychotherapy and behavior change* (pp. 257–310). New York: John Wiley.

Childress, A. C., Jarrell, M. P., & Brewerton, T. D. (1993). The Kids' Eating Disorders Survey (KEDS): Internal consistency, component analysis, and reliability. *Eating Disorders, 1,* 123–133.

Cooper, Z., & Fairburn, C. G. (1987). The Eating Disorder Examination: A semi-structured interview for the assessment of the specific psychopathology of eating disorders. *International Journal of Eating Disorders, 6*, 1–8.

Fichter, M. M., Elton, M., Engel, K., Meyer, A. E., Mall, H., & Pouska, F. (1991). Structured Interview for Anorexia and Bulimia Nervosa (SIAB): Development of a new instrument for the assessment of eating disorders. *International Journal of Eating Disorders, 10*, 571–592.

Food and Drug Administration. (2000). *Dietary supplements containing ephedrine alkaloids: Withdrawal in part* (DHHS Pub. No. 65–FR 17510). Washington, D.C.: U.S. Government Printing Office.

Garner, D. M. (1991). Eating Disorders Inventory-2. Odessa, Florida: Psychological Assessment Resources.

Garner, D. M., & Garfinkel, P. E. (1979). The Eating Attitudes Test: An index of the symptoms of anorexia nervosa. *Psychological Medicine, 9*, 273–279.

Kaplan, A. S., & Garfinkel, P. E. (1993). *Medical issues and the eating disorders: The interface*. New York: Brunner/Mazel.

Lai, K. Y., de Bruyn, R., Lask, B., Bryant-Waugh, R., & Hankins, M. (1994). Use of pelvic ultrasound to monitor ovarian and uterine maturity in childhood onset anorexia nervosa. *Archives of Disease in Childhood, 71*, 228–231.

Lask, B. (2000). Determining ideal weight [Letter to the editor]. *Eating Disorders Review, 11*, 8.

Maloney, M. J., McGuire, J. B., & Daniels, S. R. (1988). Reliability testing of a children's version of the Eating Attitudes Test. *Journal of the American Academy of Child and Adolescent Psychiatry, 27*, 541–543.

Mehler, P. S., & Andersen, A. E. (Eds.). (1999). *Eating disorders: A guide to medical care and complications*. Baltimore: Johns Hopkins University Press.

Mitchell, J. E., Pomeroy, C., & Adson, D. E. (1997). Managing medical complications. In D. M. Garner & P. E. Garfinkel (Eds.), *Handbook of treatment for eating disorders* (2nd Ed., pp. 383–393). New York: Guilford Press.

Palmer, R., Christie, M., Cordle, C., Davies, D., & Kenrick, J. (1987). The Clinical Eating Disorder Rating Instrument (CEDRI): A preliminary description. *International Journal of Eating Disorders, 6*, 9–16.

Powers, P. S. (2000). Standard laboratory and medical evaluation, *Academy for Eating Disorders Newsletter, 17(2)*, 4–5.

Reiff, D. W., & Reiff, K. L. R. (1992). *Eating disorders: Nutrition therapy in the recovery process.* Gaithersberg, Maryland: Aspen.

Thelen, M. H., Farmer, J., Wonderlich, S., & Smith, M. (1991). A revision of the Bulimia Test: The BUILT-R. *Psychological Assessment, 3*, 119–124.

Treasure, J. L., Wheeler, M., King, W. A., Gordon, P. A., & Russell, G. F. (1988). Weight gain and reproductive function: Ultrasonographic and endocrine features in anorexia nervosa. *Clinical Endocrinology, 29*, 607–616.

Williamson, D. A. (1990). *Assessment of eating disorders: Obesity, anorexia, and bulimia nervosa.* Elmsford, New York: Pergamon Press.

We hope that after reading this book the reader has gleaned a deeper understanding of how dieting can become dangerous — even deadly. As Arthur Crisp stated in the Foreword, anorexia and bulimia represent "attempted biological solutions to existential problems." In other words, our stressed and confused young people often look to their bodies to compensate for feelings of gross inadequacy. In doing so, they find perceived solutions to problems, masks to cover fears, and a physical identity to substitute for any real feeling of self. As has been amply illustrated, the ramifications can be crippling both psychologically and physically.

Fortunately, early detection and prompt, appropriate treatment can facilitate healing and result in complete recovery for many sufferers. Even after a chronic course of illness, intensive intervention with a qualified team of professionals can produce favorable results in a motivated patient. This knowledge should engender and sustain hope; people do get well from these potentially devastating diseases.

Research in the field of eating disorders is relatively young, with much remaining to be learned about causes, consequences, and treatment. The future holds promise for discoveries that will lead to still more effective prevention, detection, understanding, and clinical intervention.

Professional Resources and Organizations with Information on Eating Disorders

(Please note that websites may change over time.)

AUSTRALIA

Eating Disorders Resource Centre
53 Railway Tce
Milton, Queensland, 4064
61-07-3876-2500; *www.uq.net.au/eda/documents/start.html*

AUSTRIA

General Medical Information

www.netdoktor.at

Professional Information

www.netdoktorpro.at

CANADA

Anorexia Nervosa, British Columbia
www.anorexianervosa.org

Anorexia Nervosa and Bulimia (ANAB), Quebec
114 Donegani Boulevard
Pointe Claire, Quebec H9R 2W3
514-630-0907; *www.generation.net/~anebque/english/home.html*

National Eating Disorders Information Centre (NEDIC)
CW 1-211, 200 Elizabeth Street
M5G 2C4, Toronto
416-340-4156; *www.nedic.ca*

FINLAND

Anorexia Nervosa
www.kuh.fi/~las-web/anorexia.htm

FRANCE

Boulimie
www.boulimie.com

Centre de Traitement
www.mediom.qc.ca/~anorexie/home.htm

Encyclopedie Medico Chirurgicale (EMC)
www.emc-psychiatrie.com

Reseau Tca Ile de France
Centre Hôpitalier Sainte Anne
1, rue Cabanis
75674 Paris, Cedex 14
33-1-45-65-88-99

Something Fishy Organization (en français)
www.something~fishy.org

GERMANY

General Medical Information

www.medicine-worldwide.de

www.netdoktor.de

Bundesärztekammer
Herbert-Lewin-Strasse 1, 50931 Köln
49-0221-4004-0; *www.bundesaertztekammer.de*

Hungrig-online
www.hungrig-online.de

Magersucht-online
www.magersucht-online.de

Professional Information

www.netdoktorpro.de

Anorexia Nervosa und Bulimia Nervosa
www.uni-leipzig.de/~anorexia/index1.htm

ITALY

Associazione Italiana Disturbi dell' Alimentazione e del Peso
(AIDAP), in association with Positive Press
www.positivepress.net/aidap

Positive Press
via Sansovino, 16
37138 Verona
39-045-8102807-8103932

Associazione per lo studio e la ricerca sull'anoressia, la bulimia i
disordini alimentary l'obesita (ABA)

via Giambullari, 8   via Solferino, 14
Roma   Milano
39-02-659-659-5-02-29-000-226   39-06-70-49-19-12
www.bulimianoressia.it

THE NETHERLANDS

Bulimia-nervosa
www.bulimia-nervosa.com

Stichting Anorexia en Boulimia Nervosa
www.sabn.nl

NORWAY

General Medical Information

www.nettdoktor.no

Interessegruppa for Kvinner med Spiseforstyrrelser (IKS)
Addresses listed for Oslo, Trondheim, Sandefjord, Lillehammer/
   Hamar, Fredrikstad, Gjovik/Toten, Kristiansand, Bergen, Tromso,
   and Skien at *www.iks.no*

Professional Information

www.nettdoktor.no/pro

SPAIN

Associación contra l'Anorèxia i la Bulímia (ACAB)
Avenida Prícep d'Astúries, 5, 5e, 1a
08012 Barcelona
34-902-11-69-86
www.acab.org

Asociación Psychológica Iberoamericana de Clínica y Salud (APICSA)
Apartado de Correos
1245, 18080 Granada
www.apicsa.com

Diario Medico
www.diariomedico.com

Intersalud
www.intersalud.es/intersalud

Societat Catalana de Recerca I Terapia del Comportament (SCRTC)
Apartat de Correus 11
Universitat Autònoma de Barcelona
08193 Bellaterra (Barcelona)
www.scritc.org/ct/enlla.htm

Something Fishy Organization (en español)
www.something~fishy.org

Spanish Cognitive Behavioral Association
www.aepc.ieanet.com

Viasalus
www.viasalus.com

SWEDEN

Anorexia/Bulimia Kontakt
Regeringsgatan 88
111 39 Stockholm
46-08-20-72-14; *www.abkontakt.nu*

Anorexi-bulimi
www.medivra.se/AN

Vad ar anorexia nervosa
www.netdoktor.se

UNITED KINGDOM

Eating Disorders Association (EDA)
First floor, Wensum House
103, Prince of Wales Road
Norwich, NR1 1DW
41-01603-621-414; *www.edauk.com*

UNITED STATES

Academy for Eating Disorders (AED)
6728 Old McLean Village Drive
McLean, VA 22101-3906
703-556-9222; *www.aedweb.org*

American Academy of Child and Adolescent Psychiatry
3615 Wisconsin Avenue N.W.
Washington, DC 20016-3007
202-966-7300; *www.aacap.org/web/aacap/*

American Dietetic Association
216 W. Jackson Boulevard
Chicago, IL 60606-0040
312-899-0040
www.eatright.org

American Psychiatric Association
1400 K Street N.W.
Washington, DC 20005
888-357-7924
www.psych.org

American Psychological Association
750 First Street N.E.
Washington, DC 20002-4242
800-374-2721
www.apa.org

Anorexia Nervosa and Related Eating Disorders (ANRED)
(now affiliated with the National Eating Disorders Association)
www.anred.com

Eating Disorders Referral and Information Center
www.edreferral.com

Gurze Books
P.O. Box 2238
Carlsbad, CA 92018
800-756-7533; *www.gurze.com*

International Association of Eating Disorders Professionals (IAEDP)
P.O. Box 35882
Phoenix, AZ 85069-8552
602-934-3024; *www.iaedp.com*

National Association of Anorexia Nervosa and Associated Disorders
   (ANAD)
P.O. Box 7
Highland Park, IL 60035
847-831-3438; *www.anad.org*

National Eating Disorders Association
603 Stewart Street, Suite 803
Seattle, WA 98101
206-382-3587; *www.nationaleatingdisorders.org*

National Institutes of Health (NIH)
Building 1
1 Center Drive
Bethesda, MD 20852
301-496-4000; *www.nih.gov*

Something Fishy Organization
1104 Smithtown Avenue, Suite 121
Bohemia, NY 11716
www.something~fishy.org

appendix b

Supplemental Readings

Note: The following list of English titles is not exhaustive, but represents selected readings with which we are familiar and that we recommend. Some overlap may occur between categories. The foreign-language titles are a combination of books translated from English and texts recommended to us by our colleagues abroad.

IN ENGLISH

Anorexia Nervosa

Bruch, H. (1978). *The golden cage: The enigma of anorexia nervosa.* New York: HarperCollins.

Brumberg, J. J. (1988). *Fasting girls: The emergence of anorexia nervosa as a modern disease.* Cambridge, Massachusetts: Harvard University Press.

Crisp, A. H. (1995). *Anorexia nervosa: Let me be.* London: Academic Press.

Crisp, A. H., Joughin, N., Halek, C., & Bowyer, C. (1996). *Anorexia nervosa: The wish to change.* East Sussex, UK: Psychology Press.

Athletes and Eating Disorders

Brownell, K. D., Roding, J., & Wilmore, J. H. (Eds.). (1992). *Eating, body weight, and perfection in athletes: Disorders of modern society.* Philadelphia: Lea & Febiger.

Otis, C. L., & Goldingay, R. (2000). The athletic woman's survival guide: How to win the battle against eating disorders, amenorrhea, and osteoporosis. Champaign, Illinois: Human Kinetics.

Thompson, R. A., & Sherman, R. T. (1993). *Helping athletes with eating disorders.* Champaign, Illinois: Human Kinetics.

Binge Eating Disorder and Compulsive Overeating

Cohen, M. A. (1995). *French toast for breakfast: Declaring peace with emotional eating.* Carlsbad, California: Gurze Books.

Fairburn, C. G. (1995). *Overcoming binge eating.* New York: Guilford Press.

Hirschman, J., & Munter, C. (1988). *Overcoming overeating.* New York: Ballantine.

Roth, G. (1983). *Feeding the hungry heart.* Bergenfield, New Jersey: Penguin.

Roth, G. (1984). *Breaking free from compulsive eating.* Bergenfield, New Jersey: Penguin.

Roth, G. (1989). *Why weight: A guide to ending compulsive overeating.* Bergenfield, New Jersey: Penguin.

Body Image

Cash, T. F. (1997). *The body image workbook: An 8-step program for learning to like your looks.* Oakland, California: New Harbinger.

Freedman, R. (1988). *BodyLove: Learning to like ourselves and our looks.* New York: HarperCollins.

Hutchinson, M. G. (1985). *Transforming body image.* Freedom, California: Crossing Press.

Maine, M. (1999). *Body wars: Making peace with women's bodies in the new millennium.* Carlsbad, California: Gurze Books.

Rodin, J. (1992). *Body traps.* New York: William Morrow.

Bulimia Nervosa

Hall, L., & Cohn, L. (1999). *Bulimia: A guide to recovery.* Carlsbad, California: Gurze Books.

Schmidt, U., & Treasure, J. (1993). *Getting better bit(e) by bit(e).* East Sussex, UK: Psychology Press.

Eating Disorders — General

Chermin, K. (1985), *The hungry self: Women, eating and identity.* New York: HarperCollins.

Costin, C. (1999). *Eating disorder sourcebook: A comprehensive guide to the causes, treatments, and prevention of eating disorders,* 2nd Ed. Los Angeles: Lowell House.

Kinoy, B. (Ed.). (2001). *Eating disorders: New directions in treatment and recovery,* 2nd Ed. New York: Columbia University Press.

Lemberg, R. (Ed.), with Cohn, L. (1999). *Eating disorders: A reference sourcebook.* Phoenix, Arizona: Oryx Press.

Maine, M. (1991). *Father hunger: Fathers, daughters and food.* Carlsbad, California: Gurze Books.

Zerbe, K. J. (1995). *The body betrayed: A deeper understanding of women, eating disorders and treatment.* Washington, D.C.: American Psychiatric Press.

Eating Disorders in Children

Bryant-Waugh, R., & Lask, B. (1995). Childhood-onset eating disorders. In K. D. Brownell & C. G. Fairburn (Eds.), *Eating disorders and obesity: A comprehensive handbook* (pp. 183–187). New York: Guilford Press.

Lask, B., & Bryant-Waugh, R. (Eds.). (1993). *Childhood onset anorexia nervosa and related eating disorders.* East Sussex, UK: Lawrence Erlbaum.

Lask, B., & Bryant-Waugh, R. (1997). Prepubertal eating disorders. In D. M. Garner & P. Garfinkel (Eds.), *Handbook of treatment for eating disorders* (2nd Ed., pp. 476–483). New York: Guilford Press.

Lask, B., & Bryant-Waugh, R. (1999). *Eating disorders: A parent's guide from the Great Ormond Street Hospital Eating Disorders Clinic.* London: Penguin Books.

Lask, B., & Bryant-Waugh, R. (2000). *Anorexia nervosa and related eating disorders in childhood and adolescence* (2nd Ed.). East Sussex, UK: Psychology Press.

Eating Disorders in Males

Andersen, A. E. (1990). *Males with eating disorders.* New York: Brunner/Mazel.

Andersen, A. E., Cohn, L., & Holbrook, T. (2000). *Making weight: Healing men's conflicts with food, weight and shape.* Carlsbad, California: Gurze Books.

For Family, Friends, Teachers, and Coaches

Costin, C. (1997). *Your dieting daughter: Is she dying for attention?* New York: Brunner/Mazel.

Natenshon, A. H. (1999). *When your child has an eating disorder: A step-by-step workbook for parents and other caregivers.* San Francisco: Jossey-Bass.

Siegel, M., Brisman, J., & Weinshel, M. (1997). *Surviving an eating disorder: Perspective and strategies for families and friends* (Rev. Ed.). New York: HarperCollins.

Treasure, J. (1997). *Anorexia nervosa: A survival guide for families, friends and sufferers.* East Sussex, UK: Psychology Press.

For Professionals

Brownell, K. D., & Fairburn, C. G. (1995). *Eating disorders and obesity: A comprehensive handbook.* New York: Guilford Press.

Fairburn, C. G., & Wilson, T. (1993). *Binge eating: Nature, assessment and treatment.* New York: Guilford Press.

Fallon, P., Katzman, M., & Wooley, S. C. (1994). *Feminist perspectives on eating disorders.* New York: Guilford Press.

Garner, D., & Garfinkel, P. (Eds.). (1997). *Handbook of treatment for eating disorders* (2nd Ed.). New York: Guilford Press.

Hatch-Bruch, J. (1996). *Unlocking the golden cage: An intimate biography of Hilde Bruch.* Carlsbad, California: Gurze Books.

Johnson, C. (Ed.). (1991). *Psychodynamic treatment of anorexia nervosa and bulimia.* New York: Guilford Press.

Lask, B., and Bryant-Waugh, R. (2000). *Anorexia nervosa and related eating disorders in childhood and adolescence* (2nd Ed.). East Sussex, UK: Psychology Press.

Lemberg, R. (Ed.), with Cohn, L. (1999). *Eating disorders: A reference sourcebook.* Phoenix, Arizona: Oryx Press.

Levine, M. P., Piran, N., & Steiner-Adair, C. (Eds.). (1999). *Preventing eating disorders: A handbook of interventions and special challenges.* New York: Brunner/Routledge.

Reiff, D. W., & Reiff, K. L. R. (1992). *Eating disorders: Nutrition therapy in the recovery process.* Gaithersberg, Maryland: Aspen.

Schmidt, U., & Treasure, J. (1997). *The clinician's guide to getting better bit(e) by bit(e).* East Sussex, UK: Psychology Press.

Vandereycken, W., Kog, E., & Vanderlinden, M. A. (Eds.). (1989). *The family approach to eating disorders.* New York: PMA Publishing.

Woodside, B., Shekter-Wolfson, L., Brandes, J., & Lackstrom, J. (1993). *Eating disorders and marriage.* New York: Brunner/Mazel.

Medical Complications

American Psychiatric Association Work Group on Eating Disorders. (2000). Practice guideline for the treatment of patients with eating disorders (Rev.). *American Journal of Psychiatry, 157 (Suppl. 1),* 1–39.

Kaplan, A. S., & Garfinkel, P. (1993). *Medical issues and eating disorders: The interface.* New York: Brunner/Mazel.

Mehler, P. S., & Andersen, A. E. (Eds.). (1999). *Eating disorders: A guide to medical care and complications.* Baltimore: Johns Hopkins University Press.

Powers, P. S. (2000). Standard laboratory and medical evaluation. *Academy for Eating Disorders Newsletter, 17,* 4–5.

Zerbe, K. (Ed.). (1999). *Women's mental health in primary care.* Philadelphia: W. B. Saunders.

IN FRENCH

Bruch, H. (1990). *Conversations avec des anorexiques.* 28 fevrier.

Bruch, H. (1994). *Les yeux et le ventre: L'obese, l'anorexique.* Reed Payot: Shores (Scientific Library Payot).

Maine, M. (1995). *Anorexie, boulimie, pourquoi? Troubles de la nutrition et relation père-fille: faim du père, soif de contact.* Souffle d'Or (Parole).

Roth, G. (1995). *Oser avoir faim.* Editions de l'Homme.

Roth, G. (1999). *Lorsque manger remplace aimer.* Stanke (Hors Collection).

Schmidt, U., & Treasure, J. (1998). *La boulimie.* ESTEM.

IN GERMAN

Bruch, H. (1998). *Der goldene Käfig. Das Rätsel der Magersucht.* Fischer.

Bruch, H. (2000). *Eßtörungen.* Fischer.

Hutchinson, M. G. (2000a). *Ich bin schön. Workshop für ein positives Selbstbild.* MVG.

Hutchinson, M. G. (2000b). *Ich find mich richtig gut. 200 sichere Tipps, wie Sie sich lieben lernen.* München: Ariston.

Meerman, R., & Vandereycken, W. (1987). *Therapie der Magersucht und Bulimia nervosa.* Berlin: De Gruyter.

Roth, G. (1989). *Essen als Ersatz. Wie man den Teufelskreis durchbricht (sachbuch).* Rnb: Row ohlt.

Treasure, J. (2001). *Gemeinsam die Magersucht besiegen. Ein Leitfaden für Betroffene, Freunde, und Angehörige.* Beltz.

Vandereycken, W., & Meerman, R. (2000). *Magersucht und Bulimie: Ein Leitfaden für Betroffene und Angehörige.* Göttingen: H. Huber.

Vanderlinden, J., Norre, J., & Vandereyecken, W. (1992). *Therapie der Bulimia Nervosa. Eine praktische Anleitung.* Stuttgart: De Gruyter.

IN ITALIAN

Crisp, A. H., Jouglin, N., Halek, C., & Bowyer, C. (1997). *Il desidero di cambiare: Il primo approccio all'anoressia nervosa (la edizione).* Verona: Positive Press.

Dalle Grave, R. (1997). *Anoressia nervosa: I fatti (2a edizione).* Verona: Positive Press.

Dalle Grave, R. (2001). *Alle mie pazienti dico . . . Informazione e auto-aiuto per superare I disturbi alimentary (4a edizione)*. Verona: Positive Press.

Fairburn, C. G. (2000). *Come vincere le abbuffate: un nuovo programma scientifico (4a edizione)*. Verona: Positive Press.

Garner, D. M., & Dalle Grave, R. (1999). *Terapia cognitivo comportamentale dei disturbi dell alimentazione (la edizione)*. Verona: Positive Press.

Hall, L., & Cohn, L. (1998). *Bulimia: una guida verso la guarigione (3a edizione)*. Verona: Positive Press.

Rodin, J. (1995). *Le trappole del corpo (la edizione)*. Verona: Positive Press.

Schmidt, U., & Treasure, J. (1996). *Migliorare morso dopo morso: Un manuale disoppravvivenza per chi soffre di bulimia nervosa e disturbi de comportmento alimentare (2a edizione)*. Verona: Positive Press.

Siegel, M., Brisman, J., & Weinshel, M. (1995). *Come sopraviviere all'anoressia e alla bulimia: Strategie per famiglie e amici (2a edizione)*. Verona: Positive Press.

Vanderlinden, J. (2001). *Vincere l'anoressia nervosa: Strategie per pazienti, familiari e terapeuti (1a edizione)*. Verona: Positive Press.

IN SPANISH

Chinchilla, A. (1996). *Guía teórico-práctica de los trastornos de la conducta alimentaira: Anorexia y bulimia nerviousa*. Barcelona: Masson.

Fernández-Aranda, F., & Turón-Gil, V. (Eds.). (1998). *Guía básica de tratamiento en anorexia y bulimia*. Barcelona: Masson.

Garcia-Camba, E. (Ed.). (2001). *Avances en trastornos de la conducta alimentaria: Anorexia, bulimia nervosa, obesidad*. Barcelona: Masson.

Hall, L., & Cohn, L. (2001). *Cómo entender y superar la bulmia*. Carlsbad, California: Gurze Books.

Morandé, G. (1995). *Un peligro llamado anorexia: La tentación de adelgazar*. Madrid: Temas de Hoy.

Roth, G. (2001). *Cuando la comida sustituye al amor*. Barcelona: Urano.

Saldaña, C. (1994). *Trastornos del comportamiento alimentario*. Madrid: Fundación Universidad Empresa.

Turón, V. J. (1996). *Trastornos de la alimentación: Anorexia nerviosa, bulimia y obesidad*. Barcelona: Masson.